SAFFRON AWAKENING

Ayodhya to Adityanath

Prafull Goradia

Vitasta
LET KNOWLEDGE SPREAD

Published by
Renu Kaul Verma
Vitasta Publishing Pvt Ltd
2/15, Ansari Road, Daryaganj
New Delhi - 110 002
info@vitastapublishing.com

ISBN 9789386473219

First Edition 2018

2nd Reprint 2023

MRP ₹ 595

Cover and layout by Vits Press
Printed by Vikas Computer and Printers

Contents

Why This Book

Over the last few years, many a member of the polity has alleged—on television as well as in person—that an atmosphere of intolerance prevails in the country. They have implicitly blamed the governments which they feel are pro-Hindu. Most of these complainants have been brought up and educated in the Macaulay-introduced culture and do not empathise with the central ethos of our country, nor with the common people of India who have voted these governments into power. A good example of this is the result (11 March 2017) of the Uttar Pradesh assembly elections, which show that the complainants are misled. Because they are intellectual, it is best to guide them back into the mainstream with the help of a book which explains what Hinduness is all about; its wisdom, its philosophy, its culture, its glories, its sufferings, its strength, its weakness.

For, those dominantly influenced by Western education and thinking find it difficult to appreciate that a religion is not always set by an authoritative book like the Bible with a monopolistic god and a network of clergy. Such a religion is a piece of deductive logic wherein the premise is given and believed by the faithful. The rituals and practices are corollaries of the premise.

Once it is accepted that Allah is the only God, the logic of Islam flows down flawlessly to the last detail. Hinduism, on the other hand, is an example of inductive logic which begins on the ground and moves upwards. Each ground can be different from the other, which in turn leads to differing conclusions; there being no premise.

For example, what happens if four Hindus from different corners of the country happen to meet and talk about roses? The man from the north might have seen roses to be red, the southerner could have seen only white ones. The easterner might identify roses as always yellow and the man from the west only pink. After a debate, it is likely that they would adjourn having agreed to disagree. In contrast, a member of an Abrahamic religion would assert that what he knows to be a rose is of only one colour. The other three are not roses; but possibly other flowers or even weeds. Such a person, therefore cannot instinctively understand the Hindu viewpoint. It is often described as a way of life.

It is so and much more, an exhaustive explanation of life, how to live it and what to expect after death. Little that is essential is left out.

The 11 March Uttar Pradesh (UP) assembly elections can be aptly called the Battle of Panipat in reverse. No blood was shed but the electoral battle is nevertheless likely to bring a turnaround in the course of Indian history. No poll in India since 1946, which led to the Partition, has been as consequential as the one in UP. Never before have the Hindus declared as loudly that it is *they* who propose to choose the destiny of their State. The assertion was not expected to be so loud and clear, although the 2014 Lok Sabha poll had been a rehearsal.

The people of UP comprise about one-fifth of all Indians.

Their electoral declaration, therefore, is a weighty one. Uttar Pradesh is also the State which has taken a great deal of battering at the hands of Muslim invaders. Vrindavan's Gobind Dev temple was literally cut into half so that the *'kafir* (infidel)' *mashaal*[1] on its roof could no longer be visible to Aurangzeb at Delhi. Krishna *janmabhoomi* or birthplace at Mathura was vandalised repeatedly, beginning with Mahmud of Ghazni in 1017 and ending with Aurangzeb six centuries later. Today, there is an Idgah on top of the birthplace and Krishna sits below in what once could have been a servant's quarter. Banaras (now Varanasi) is a similar story with the Kashi Viswanath or the most venerated temple of Lord Shiva. At its original site stands the GyanVapi mosque. There were many other temple desecrations. For example, Jaunpur in eastern UP is littered with mandirs converted into masjids and the Quwwat-ul-Islam mosque in Delhi was built with debris of 29 destroyed temples.

BR Ambedkar (Volume 8 of his writings, Chapter 4) has extensively written about how Mahmud of Ghazni began his plunderous and destructive raids on India as early as 1001 AD. He died in 1030 AD, but within the span of 30 years, he invaded India 17 times. He was followed by Mohammad Ghori who began his career as an invader in 1173, and continued till he was killed in 1206. For thirty years Ghazni had ravaged India and for thirty years Ghori inflicted the same tyranny on the country in much the same way. Being rich and fertile, UP was an attractive area to plunder. The early Turkic invaders were followed by the Mongol hordes of Chenghiz Khan. They first came in 1221, only wintering on the borders of India at first. Twenty years later, they marched inland. Of all the Islamic inroads, the most terrible was under Taimur in 1398. After him, the next invader was Babar from Uzbekistan, who invaded

1 The beacon light atop temples.

India in 1526. The invasions of India did not stop with him. There occurred two more attacks. In 1739, Nadir Shah's hordes swept over the Punjab like a flooded river 'furious as the ocean'. He was followed by Ahmad Shah Abdali who invaded India in 1761, inflicting a defeat on the Marathas at Panipat, causing a huge setback to the attempt of the Hindus to regain the ground they had lost to Muslim invaders, as Ambedkar has lamented.

There is no doubt that desecrating and destroying Hindu idols and temples and establishing Islam in India was also one of the aims of these expeditions. Mahmud of Ghazni also looked upon his numerous invasions of India as the 'waging of a jihad'. Mohammed Ghori was actuated by the same zeal in his invasions of India. Hasan Nizami, the historian, describes his work in the following terms:

> He purged by his sword the land of Hind from the filth of infidelity and vice, and freed the whole of that country from the thorn of god-plurality and the impurity of idol worship, and by his royal vigour and intrepidity left not one temple standing.

What is, however, important to bear in mind is that despite all their internecine conflicts, Muslim invaders were united by one common objective and that was to destroy the Hindu faith. For example, Ghazni from the outset acted in a manner so as to strike terror into the hearts of the Hindus. After the defeat of Raja Jaipal in 1001 AD, Mahmud ordered that he be paraded about in the streets so that his sons and chieftains might see him in that condition of shame, bondage and disgrace; and that fear of Islam might permeate the country of the infidels. The slaughtering of kafirs seemed to be one thing that gave Mahmud particular pleasure. In one attack on Chand Rai, in 1019 AD, many infidels were slain or taken prisoner, and the Muslims paid no regard to booty until they had satiated themselves with the slaughter of the Hindus.

Throughout the reign of the Mughals, we read of the destruction of temples. During Shah Jahan's time, temples that the Hindus had started to rebuild too were targeted. Accounts of this direct attack on the piety of the Hindus are thus solemnly recorded in the *Badshahnamah*:

> It had been brought to the notice of His Majesty, says the historian, that during the late reign (of Akbar) many idols and temples had been begun but remained unfinished at Banaras. The kafirs were now desirous of completing them. His Majesty, the defender of the faith, gave orders that at Banaras and throughout his dominions, all temples that had been begun should be cast down. It was reported from the province of Allahabad that 76 temples had been destroyed.

Speaking of the levy of *jaziya* (a protection tax non-Muslims living under Islamic rule must pay merely to be allowed to live), Murray Thurston Titus (an American who taught history and was later Principal of Reid Christian College, Lucknow) says:

> The payment of the jaziya by the Hindus continued throughout the dominions of the sultans in various parts of India with more or less regularity. It was abolished throughout the Mughal Empire for a while in the ninth year of Akbar's reign (1565 AD), only to be re-imposed when Aurangzeb came to power.

The methods Islamic invaders adopted have left their aftermath. One particular legacy is the bitterness between Hindus and Muslims. This is so deep-seated that even centuries of non-rule have not succeeded in assuaging it. Sir Percival Griffiths, a scholar and a retired English ICS officer, in his book *The British Impact on India,* has commented: 'In philosophy, ceremonial, the way of life they engender, and in their effect on character, no two religions could be further apart than Hinduism and Islam.'

> All what has been noted above over the centuries (Titus has summarized this to be for 762 years)has been seared into the collective memory of the Hindus. They were however, not expressed even after the British rule began. The fear of the Muslim was so deep that even an impartial rule did not bring it out. After Independence came the Nehruvian rule which pampered the Muslims. Hence, the equation between the two communities was virtually back to square one.

Until the advent of Narendra Modi, no leader was able to inspire the Hindu confidence for their true sentiments to get expression. The general election of 2014 gave an indication of great relief when 278 BJP and 57 supporting party (National Democratic Alliance) candidates were elected to the Lok Sabha. This proved to be a precursor for the outburst of Hindu voting in the Assembly election in UP in 2017. Never before has the Hindu expressed himself with such vengeance. It is a turning point in Indian history.

A Hindu, not converted to Macaulayism or at least largely uninfluenced by it will understand this difference readily. Indians who feel oppressed by supposed intolerance can benefit by familiarising themselves with Hinduness and then appreciate how a revolution carries with it its own pain. Hence several chapters beginning with *Su-raaj* or good governance have been included to give an insight into the Hindu psychology and why he tolerated the tyranny for so many centuries before reacting.

Macaulayism is not the only factor which has stood between some members of the Indian elite and the Hindu ethos. He came on the Indian scene less than 200 years ago. Before that, for some six centuries, the environment was encroached upon by Islamic beliefs backed by the rulers, especially in northern India. It was unfortunate that even after Independence, the rulers were unsympathetic to Hinduness. Jawaharlal Nehru reportedly once called himself the English prime minister of India while Sardar Patel said that Jawaharlal was the only nationalist Muslim he had come across. The cultural pace he set for 17 years as head of government, more or less, sustained for the next 50 years. The Nehruvian momentum was halted only as late as 2014 when Narendra Modi came to power in Delhi. Until then, most Indians avoided using the word Hindu lest they be misunderstood as being communal. Little wonder that Hinduness did not have any chance till then to assert itself.

In December 1992, the Babri edifice at Ayodhya was demolished. The Indian elite almost unanimously condemned the incident. Hardly anyone said that most simple Hindus believe that the spot was the birthplace of Ramchandra. So deep and wide is the belief that if I were an Indian Muslim, I would say to the Hindu: take the spot where the edifice stood and give my community compensation elsewhere.

It was uncanny that the Hindu secular opinion was more vociferous in condemning the demolition than the Muslim. No one apparently bothered to assess the historical significance of the event. The top BJP leadership was so confused that it distanced the party from the demolition. Yet it is the Hindu mass confidence that before long brought the Bharatiya Janata Party to power in Delhi for the first time in 1998. This is only to underline how much the Hindu elite has been brainwashed by centuries of alien influences, whether Islamic or English, that it has little idea of how the masses feel and think.

Jinnah wanted Muslims to Emigrate

The startling UP election results of 2017 would not have been, had Gandhiji lent his ear to the Muslim League. Its proposal for partition had included an exchange of population: most Muslims were to emigrate to Pakistan and all Hindus and Sikhs come away to Hindustan. In fact, the exchange was integral part of their demand. Partition was for Muslims to have their Dar-ul-Islam (land ruled by Islam) where they could live and flourish with the writ of the *Shariah* running throughout their land.

While addressing the Muslim League MLAs of Bihar, Sir Feroze Khan Noon, who later rose to be Prime Minister, had on 8 April 1946, threatened to reenact the murderous orgies of Genghis Khan and Halaqu Khan if non-Muslims took up an obstructive attitude against population exchange. Ismail Chundrigar, who also eventually rose to be Prime Minister of Pakistan, had said that the British had no right to hand over Muslims to a subject people over whom they had ruled for 500 years. Mohammad Ismail, a leader from Madras, had declared that the Muslims of India were in the midst of a jihad.

MA Jinnah, while addressing a press conference at Karachi on 25 November 1946, said that the authorities, both central and provincial, should immediately take up the question of exchange of population, as reported by *Dawn*, on 26 November, 1946. Shaukat Hayat Khan, son of the Prime Minister of Punjab Sir Sikander Hayat Khan, had threatened, while the British were still in India, of a rehearsal of what the Muslims would do to the Hindus eventually.

For the Muslim leaders, therefore, the idea of a population transfer was neither novel nor surprising. Even Prophet Muhammad had undertaken *hijrat* from Mecca to Medina while founding Islam. Not surprisingly, Khan Iftikhar Hussain of Mamdot had said that the exchange of population offered a very practical solution for the problem of the Muslims, reported by *Dawn* (3 December 1946). Pir Ilahi Bux, the Sindhi leader, had said that he welcomed an exchange of population for the safety of the minorities, as it would put an end to all communal disturbances as reported by *Dawn* (4 December 1946). So also felt Raja Ghazanfar Ali, who later became Pakistan's envoy to New Delhi. The *Dawn* of 19 December 1946 reported his having asked for the alteration of the population map of India. His detailed plea is reproduced in a clipping given in this chapter.

What the politicians said was confirmed by Vice-Chancellor M Mujeeb, of Jamia Millia Islamia in his erudite work, *Indian Muslims.* He said that the League demanded the creation of a separate homeland. He further stated that in the 1946 elections held early that year, the League, whose dominant manifesto was the creation of Pakistan, secured 425 seats out of 492 reserved for Muslims. The League insisted that the right to a separate homeland should be conceded first. All other negotiations could be held thereafter.

These thoughts were no doubt unsavoury to the Hindus,

but the League leaders had a clear plan. Their demand for not only partition but also population transfer had been thought through along with the implications of creating Pakistan. If a division was to be made, it had to be thorough and comprehensive. The League demand for an exchange of population was loudly voiced and widely debated. Merely to get a flavour of the contemporary reports, one may read a few clippings from the 1946 issues of the *Dawn*. It was a daily then published from Delhi and now from Karachi. The newspaper had been founded by Jinnah.

Theologically, partition was consistent with Muslim separatism, or his inability to coexist with people of other faiths. In the words of MJ Akbar (in his book *The Shade of Swords,* Roli Books, New Delhi, 2002):

> The community did not forget that Prophet Mohammad himself had warned that there should never be two religions in Arabia. In their 1,400-year history, Muslims have shown clear preference for being masters or rulers. When and wherever this has not been possible the inclination has been to migrate or undertake hijrat to another land which they could call Dar-ul-Islam or a society where the writ of the Sharia runs without any hindrance.
>
> In the absence of a Dar-ul-Islam, the Muslim feels that he would be unable to blossom as a *momin* which means a faithful. In India, since the sun finally set on the Mughal empire in 1858, Muslims have been uncomfortable. Instead of being rulers, they became British subjects like the rest of Indians. When the British were preparing to give up their Indian empire 90 years later, Muslims feared that the Hindu majority would overwhelm them. The only alternative, therefore, was partition and for that one-third of the *ummah* who would remain on the Indian side of the dividing border, hijrat was the way. To make space for the *Mohajirs*, the government of Pakistan cleared the western

wing of their country of nearly all non-Muslims on the morrow of the vivisection.

To show how this inspiration to separatism is embedded in the theology of Islam, it is useful to quote a contract that was signed between Caliph Umar II and the Jews and Christians of Arabia sometime between 717 and 720 AD. They affirmed:

- We shall not build in our cities or in their vicinity any new monasteries, churches, hermitages or monks' cells. We shall not restore by night or by day any of these that have fallen into ruin or which are located in the Muslims' quarters.
- We shall keep our gates wide open for the passersby and travellers. We shall provide three days' food and lodging to any Muslim who passes our way.
- We shall not shelter any spy in our churches or in our homes nor shall we hide him from the Muslims.
- We shall not teach our children the Qur'an.
- We shall not hold public religious ceremonies. We shall not seek to proselytise anyone. We shall not prevent any of our kin from embracing Islam if they so desire.
- We shall show deference to the Muslims and shall rise from our seats when they wish to sit down.
- We shall not attempt to resemble the Muslims in any way. We shall not ride on saddle.
- We shall not wear swords or bear weapons of any kind, or even carry them with us.
- We shall not sell wines.
- We shall clip the forelocks of our head.
- We shall not display our books anywhere in the Muslim thoroughfares or in their marketplaces. We shall only beat

our clappers in our churches very quietly. We shall not raise our voices when reciting the service in our churches, nor when in the presence of Muslims. Neither shall we raise our voices in our funeral processions.

- We shall not build our homes higher than theirs.

Instead of insisting that the kafirs or infidels subject themselves to conversion and become Muslim, or face the blade of the sword, this was a concession made to the Jews and the Christians because they were also *Ahl-e-Kitab* or the 'People of the Book' who shared common prophets. Incidentally, this privilege of not being forced to convert was only provided to those who accepted the status of a *dhimmi* or a protected citizen and paid jaziya or the poll tax. The facility was also extended to Hindus. This contract of Umar II was in tune with the Quran and the *Sunna,* or the practice of the Prophet.

To realists, it is a mystery as to why the Muslims of undivided India insisted on partition. The areas that went into Pakistan were already Muslim majority. The community there was having its way as the premiers were Muslim, be it Baluchistan, Bengal, NWFP, Punjab or Sind. All the other provinces had Hindu majorities and therefore the Muslims there could possibly ask for safeguards. After partition, prima facie they could be in a weaker situation. With the *ashras* (elite) migrating, the *ajlas* (non-elite) lost many of their patrons. This was known and was obvious to most people at the time. Yet the Muslims of UP, and to an extent those of Bihar and the Bombay Presidency, were at the forefront of the agitation for Pakistan.

A particularly noteworthy book in this context, published recently is *Creating a New Medina* by Venkat Dhulipala (Cambridge University Press), which offers a clue to this paradox. Muslims, inspired by ideologues at the Aligarh Muslim University, were anxious to create a replacement for the fallen headquarters of Islam at Istanbul. The Caliphate was based there until Kemal Mustafa abolished the institution and exiled the Caliph-cum-Sultan. Aligarh's students felt Pakistan would be the ideological centre of global Islam. Even if the Muslims remaining in India happened to suffer, the sacrifice would be well worthwhile for the cause of Islam.

Author Dhulipala has quoted at considerable length what Maulana Shabbir Ahmad Usmani of Bijnore (UP) had advocated. He glorified Pakistan as the first Islamic state in history that would attempt to reconstruct the Islamic utopia created by the Prophet in Medina. He constantly used Pakistan and Medina interchangeably to solidify their identification in the public mind.

Little wonder that Justice MC Chagla (*Roses in December*), Rafiq Zakaria (*The Man who Divided India*) and the Aga Khan (autobiography) have all blamed Aligarh University for being the ideological cradle of Pakistan. Qaid-e-Azam Jinnah called it the 'arsenal of Pakistan!' Sir Syed Ahmad Khan was the first prophet of partition when in a speech at Lucknow in 1887 and again at Meerut in 1888 he declared that Hindus and Muslims were separate nations.

Partition, however, was not entirely ideology-inspired. For example, the Shias, whose spiritual and temporal head was the Caliph, were not integrally a part of the ummah. Whoever became a Shia was and is the follower of Hazrat Ali and his son Husain, who was cheated out of the Caliphate he was promised by Muaviah and his son Yazid, the fifth and sixth Caliphs. Following the butchery of Husain and his male relatives at Karbala in 680 AD, schism set in between Sunnis and Shias. The latter believe in their Imams while the former looked up to the Caliphs. Jinnah was a Shia and yet his unquestioned leadership led to partition; he is rightly called the founder of Pakistan (who had supported neither the Khilafat movement nor the establishment of Aligarh University).

The Muslims of the Bombay Presidency enthusiastically

supported Jinnah and his movement. Of them, the Khojas and Bohras are Shia while the Memons are Sunni. They were the leading financiers of the Muslims League. For example, the Habib family (Khoja) had all its business and assets in Bombay. Yet they wholeheartedly backed the partition. His grain business partner Ratilal Gandhi, who was also for several years the president of Bombay Pradesh Congress, asked him the reason for this. The Habibs' answer was simple. In Pakistan, the Khojas would have to compete with the Punjabi farmer. While in India, they were up against the Parsi industrialists, the Banias, the Marwaris, the Chettiars et al. Jinnah also had his own vested interest as told to my grandfather Dharamdas Vora whose close friend was Ahmed Ali, the Qaid's younger brother. According to Ahmed, his elder brother had to be number one wherever he be. If he could not be the *badshah* of the whole of India, he would rather be the sultan of a part of it. He had to have his place in the hall of fame.

Coming back to population transfer, the idea goes back to Spain of 1609 AD when Moriscos, the Moors or Muslims of Spanish origin were expelled because they refused to reconvert to Christianity. They were resettled in Algeria, Morocco and Tunisia. Next, some four lakh Protestants were asked by King Louis XIV to leave France; they resettled in England, Prussia, Holland and America. These precedents of population transfer are based on a book by Stephen P Ladas called *The Exchange of Minorities* (Macmillan Company, New York, 1932). It may have given ideas to Jinnah as well as Ambedkar to develop their views on the exchange.

In the 20th century, the Treaty at Neuilly was signed in France soon after the end of World War I. Among its several terms Bulgaria and Greece exchanged their ethnic minorities living in each others' territory. In 1923, Lord Curzon, on behalf of the League of Nations (like the UNO but of post-World War I) supervised the signing of the Treaty of Lausanne between

Greece and Turkey. It provided for the free and spontaneous emigration of Greek Muslims and Turkish Christians to the two respective countries. The properties of the emigrants were appraised and disposed of. The exchange would not prejudice the rights of property and monetary assets of the exchanged people. They were to be free to take away or arrange for the transport of their movable property. They could also leave behind property, in which case the local authorities were to draw up an inventory and valuation of such property. Immovable and movable property of the exchanged populations was to be sold off by the Mixed (or joint) Commission.

The convention of 30 January 1923, regarding the exchange of Greek and Turkish populations, was a part of the peace settlement with Turkey. It was proposed that the exchange should be carried out within three months. Lord Curzon, the British Foreign Secretary, expressed his preference for *a compulsory exchange*, as only in this way could the expected results be obtained. The sums due to the exchanged population of each country on account of the property liquidated by the Mixed Commission was to constitute a government debt from the country where the liquidation took place, to the government of the country to which the proprietors emigrated. The exchanged populations were entitled, in principle, to receive in their new country property of a value equal to and of the same nature as that which they had left behind. Provisions were made for settlement of accounts between the two governments as a result of the liquidation (Article 14 of the Treaty).

The Muslim League resolved to demand partition on 23 March 1940. BR Ambedkar soon set about thinking through the ramifications of creating partition. The author of this book has not come across anyone who thought as sincerely about the security of Hindus as Ambedkar did. What he wrote gives an insight into what Ambedkar thought of partition six or seven years before it took place. He proved remarkably prescient. Had we listened to him, we would not have suffered the communal tension and the virtual repeat of a hundred years ago.

By 1941, Ambedkar's detailed work entitled *Pakistan or the Partition of India* was in the market. Much later in 1990, the book was reprinted as part of Ambedkar's complete works by the government of Maharashtra. It formed Volume 8 of the comprehensive publication. The chapters in this book largely consist of extracts from that book. Ambedkar was one of the few people who recommended partition for the sake of Hindu safety and India's military security. Apart from the inevitable vivisection of territory, he strongly advocated an exchange of population. The Muslims on the Indian side were to emigrate to Pakistan and non-Muslims from Pakistani territory were to come away to this side of the border. Ambedkar did not consider the transfer unduly difficult and quoted the precedents of Bulgaria, Greece and Turkey.

How would the creation of Pakistan affect the defence of Hindustan? This question was posed by Babasaheb from the viewpoints of frontiers, of resources, of the armed forces, of communal peace, of redrawing of boundaries.

It is a feature which, if widely known, will set many people thinking furiously. It is sure to raise questions that may prove insoluble and may easily block the path of India's political progress. Yet another particular feature of the Indian army of the 1930s was the much-overlooked question of communal composition. One Mr Chaudhari, a military expert quoted by Ambedkar, has highlighted this aspect. The following table shows the proportion of soldiers serving in the Indian infantry, according to the area and the community from which they were drawn in the 1930s:

> Two glaring facts stand out from this survey. The first is that the Indian army is predominantly Muslim in its composition. The other is that Musalmans who predominate are from the Punjab and the NWFP. Such a composition

Area and Communities in 1930	%age
I. **The NWFP, Punjab and Kashmir**	**58.5**
Sikhs Punjabi (Hindus—Ed.) Musalmans Pathans (Muslims—Ed.)	13.58 22.6 6.55
II. Nepal, Kumaon, Garhwal	**22.00**
Gurkhas (Hindus—Ed.)	16.4
III. Upper India	**11.0**
UP Rajputs (Hindus—Ed.) Hindustani (Hindus—Ed.) Musalmans Brahmins (Hindus—Ed.)	 2.55 Nil Nil
IV. South India	**5.5**
Mahrattas (Hindus—Ed.) Madrasi (Hindus—Ed.) Musalmans Tamils (Hindus—Ed.)	 5.33 Nil Nil

means that the Musalmans have been made the principal defenders of India from foreign invasion. And they are conscious of this proud position which has been assigned to them by the British. One often hears them say that they are the gate-keepers of India. The Hindus must consider the problem of the defence of India in this light. How far can the Hindus depend upon these gatekeepers to hold the gate and protect the liberty and freedom of India? The behaviour of the Indian soldier under British control is artificial. His behaviour when he is under Indian control would be his natural behaviour. British control does not allow much play to the natural instincts and sympathies of men. That is why the men in the army behave so well. The realist must take note of the fact that Musalmans look upon Hindus as kafirs, who deserve to be exterminated rather than protected. The realist must take note of the fact that while Musalmans accept the European as his superior, he looks upon the Hindu as his inferior. It is doubtful how far a regiment of Musalmans will accept the authority of Hindu officers if it be placed under them. The realist must take note that of all the Musalmans, the ones from the North-West are the most disaffected in their relations with Hindus. The realist must take note that the Punjabi Musalman is fully susceptible to the propaganda in favour of pan-Islamism.

The views held by the Mohammedans (certainly the most aggressive and truculent of the peoples of India) are alone sufficient to prevent the establishment of an independent Indian Government. Were the Afghan to descend from the north upon an autonomous India, the Mohammedans, instead of uniting with the Sikhs and the Hindus to repel him, would be drawn by all the ties of kinship and religion to join his flag.

Hindus have a difficult choice to make: to have a safe army or a safe border? Is it in their interest to insist that Muslim India should remain part of India so that they may have a safe border, or is it in their interest to welcome its separation from India so that they may have a safe army? Which is then better for the Hindus? Should the Musalmans be without and against or should they be within and against? If the question is asked of any prudent man, there will be only one answer, namely, that if the Musalmans are to be against the Hindus, it is better that they should be without and against, rather than within and against. Indeed, it is a consummation devoutly to be wished that the Muslims should be without. That is the only way of getting rid of the Muslim preponderance in the Indian army.

How can it be brought about? Here again, there is only one way to bring it about and that is to support the scheme for creating Pakistan. Once Pakistan is created, Hindustan, having ample resources of men and money, can have an army which it can call its own and there will be nobody to dictate as to how it should be used and against whom it should be used. The defence of Hindustan, far from being weakened by the creation of Pakistan, would be infinitely improved.

The Pakistan area, which is the main recruiting ground of the present Indian army, contributes very little to the central exchequer as will be seen from the following figures: The Pakistan provinces, it will be seen, contribute very little. The main contribution comes from the provinces of Hindustan. In fact, it is the money contributed by the provinces of Hindustan which enables the Government of India to carry out its activities in Pakistan provinces. The latter are a drain on the former. Not only do they contribute very little to the central government, instead they receive a great deal from the centre. The revenue of the central government amounts to Rs 121 crore, of this about Rs 52 crore are spent annually on the army. In what area is this amount spent? Who pays the bulk of this amount of Rs 52 crore, which is spent on the Muslim army drawn from the Pakistan area? It is contributed by Hindu provinces and is spent on an army which consists mainly of non-Hindus! How many Hindus are aware of this tragedy? How many know at whose cost this tragedy

Contribution to the Central Exchequer[2]	**Rs**
Punjab North-West Frontier Sind Baluchistan	11,801,385 928,294 58,646,915 Nil
Total	**71,376,594**
As against this, the provinces of Hindustan contribute as follows:	**Rs**
Madras Bombay Bengal UP Bihar CP&Berar Assam Orissa	95,326,745 225,344,247 120,000,000 40, 553,000 15,437,742 3,142,682 18,755,967 567,346
Total	**519,127,729**

is being enacted? Today the Hindus are not responsible because they cannot prevent it. The question is whether they will allow this tragedy to continue. If they mean to stop it, the surest way of putting an end to it is to allow a Pakistan to come into being. To oppose it is to buy a sure weapon for their own destruction.

Only if such a population transfer had been agreed upon by Indian leaders, Gandhi and Jawaharlal Nehru particularly, India would not still be suffering communal tensions. It is relevant here to quote what Syama Prasad Mookerjee had to tell Parliament on 15 November 1952. Wave after wave of refugees were coming in from East Pakistan and the

---

2 Pre-World War II Figures: Only 50% revenue is shown because nearly 1/2 the population is Hindu.

government in Delhi was doing little about them. Mookerjee recalled how, accompanied by Rajkumari Amrit Kaur, he went to see Gandhi a few weeks before his death. He had this to say:

> We were discussing this question. He came out with fire in his eyes. He (Gandhi) said: 'We did not agree to the partition of India for this terrible rehabilitation causing misery to millions of people: it was on a certain fundamental basis: the minorities must be protected; they must live in their own homeland: no question of their being turned out as beggars.' What was his remedy? He said: 'Let India play her part; you protect the minorities: let not one man be turned out from here; then turn towards Pakistan and say we have fulfilled our part, but you have not; it becomes a world problem; it becomes a moral problem.' The words which he uttered are still ringing in my ears. He said: 'If Pakistan fails to do so, if there is no other remedy you must take charge of East Bengal; let government take charge and protect the people.' He added: 'I cannot join the war, I do not believe in it; but I will bless you that you have the moral courage for it. [I] will remember that. I am not advocating war: but if there is no other means of protecting the minorities of East Pakistan except to take charge of that territory, Government of India will someday have to consider it. I am not using [the] word lightly; I am not saying that immediately war should be declared. It would not be necessary also. There was no war in Hyderabad. They are not ready for war. Goondaism does not wish to face war. They want to gain something without sacrifice.' Only if the Prime Minister says Government will act firmly and adopts a policy not of weakness and appeasement you will see what happens. He is proud of appeasement. I am amazed at it. He may say, I cannot find a solution: I can sympathise with that. But he glorifies appeasement and

> goes on appeasing; at whose cost? If he does it at his cost…

In 1946, Rajendra Prasad, President of India for the first two terms, happened to comment on the Pakistan demand of the Muslim League. His book was called *India Divided,* to which he subsequently added an *Addendum.* Therein he quotes an interview of Jinnah by Donald Edwards of the BCC and simultaneously comments. A relevant portion is reproduced below:

> A question has been engaging public attention ever since the two-nation theory was propounded. All Muslims being one nation by reason of their religion alone, irrespective of any other considerations like the territory they inhabit, the language they speak etc., the question naturally arises what would be the position and status of the Muslims who will be left in Hindustan, which according to the League proposal will be a Hindu state. Jinnah, on being asked what he proposed for those areas where the Muslims are in a minority replied in the course of the interview referred to above:
>
> 'Those areas, like Madras for instance, will have a Hindu government and the Muslim minority there will have three courses open to them: they may accept citizenship of the state in which they are; they can remain there as foreigners; or they can come to Pakistan. I will welcome them. There is plenty of room. But it is for them to decide.'
>
> Jinnah accepts the position that the Muslims who are citizens of India today will, after Partition, cease to be citizens of Hindustan and therefore they will have three alternatives to choose from. Let us examine these three alternatives.
>
> The first alternative is that they may accept citizenship in the state in which they are. It may be pointed out that citizenship can be acquired by a foreigner in a state only

under rules made for that purpose by the state concerned. It is open to any state which is independent to regulate and control its own population and to lay down restrictions on foreigners acquiring citizenship and even to prohibit it altogether. The history of the British Dominions like South Africa, Canada and Australia, which are all members of the British Commonwealth and Empire, to which India also belongs, and which owe allegiance to the same King-emperor to whom Indians are in law required to owe allegiance, shows how they have successfully and effectively prevented Indians from acquiring the rights of citizenship. The United States of America also regulates immigration and does not permit any and every foreigner to acquire the right of citizenship simply because the foreigner wishes to have that right. So, if Hindustan is to be really a free and sovereign state, it will have the same right to regulate its citizenship and to lay down rules for and even to prohibit acquisition of the rights of citizenship by foreigners. It will not lie with the Muslims left in Hindustan to become its citizens unless Hindustan permits it. Jinnah, of course, assumes that Hindus must not be allowed to put difficulties in their way.

The second alternative is that they can remain there as foreigners. Here again he makes the same assumption. Hindustan, like any other independent state, will not be bound to allow foreigners to remain on its territory, particularly when they happen to be in such large numbers as the Muslims will be. It is also worth remembering that an independent state may regulate and even prohibit the acquisition of property, particularly immovable property, by foreigners within its territory.

The third alternative is that the Musalmans who will be left in Hindustan can go to Pakistan. This, of course, is legally possible. Every foreigner is entitled to leave the foreign state and to go to his own state.

In short, Rajendra Prasad's view was that because the partition was on the basis of a single criterion, namely, Islam, the Muslims who wish to stay back in Hindustan could do so as aliens by obtaining visas, not as citizens. Or else, they must undertake hijrat (migration) to the Dar-ul-Islam, namely Pakistan or the New Medina.

Uttar Pradesh Since 1952

Transformation of Electoral Landscape

The electoral history of Uttar Pradesh begins with the heydays of the sway of the Congress over the State, which, as the years went by, was gradually eclipsed first by regional casteist satraps and then by an increasingly assertive Hindu nationalism. The 2017 assembly election in UP has seen the BJP gain total domination in the State, while the once mighty Congress has been reduced to a footnote. It has also been a saga of the marginalisation of the Muslim vote, which all parties except the BJP wooed in order to grab power. UP 2017, a victory scripted by the persona and leadership of Modi, has made the Muslim vote—and veto—irrelevant. The consequences will be far-reaching.

Independent India, reeling under the trauma of partition, held its first-ever general election in 1952.

The first UP State assembly that came into being had 425 seats. Uttarakhand was then part of UP. In the election of 1952, the Congress won 388 of them. Congress stalwart Pandit Govind Ballabh Pant was already the Chief Minister of UP, and merely continued in the post. He remained chief minister until December 1954, when he moved to Delhi to become the Union Home Minister. Pant was succeeded by Sanskrit scholar Sampoornanand from Varanasi. Despite a near-total dominance of the State by the Congress, its internal bickering began in the mid-1950s.

The Congress won the 1957 elections, but Sampoornanand could stay on as chief minister only until 1960. Another emerging party stalwart, Kamlapati Tripathi, soon began gunning for him. Sampoornanand had to vacate the State's throne for Chandra Bhanu Gupta, who too did not complete his term. Sucheta Kriplani, the wife of Acharya JB Kriplani, replaced Gupta in 1963, becoming the first woman Chief Minister of Uttar Pradesh.

The period of 1951-67 can be called the age of Congress dominance, but one could say that the seeds of its eventual fall were sown in this very decade.

1967 happened to be the year when Hindu nationalism, till then dormant, began asserting itself. Its political visage became apparent in Uttar Pradesh that year. To Charan Singh went the credit of forming the first non-Congress government in UP after the 1967 election, but it was the Bharatiya Jana Sangh, precursor of the BJP, which made a notable entry in the polity of Uttar Pradesh that year.

The Congress tally fell to 199—short of majority in the 425 seat Assembly—while the Jana Sangh won 98 seats. Kriplani went to Lok Sabha, while Chandra Bhanu Gupta scraped through at the Ranikhet assembly seat by just 72 votes. Jat leader Chaudhary Charan Singh won the Chhaproli seat by over 52,000 votes, and then broke with the Congress to form his Bhartiya Kranti Dal (BKD). He was backed by socialists Ram Manohar Lohia and Raj Narain, and the Jana Sangh's Nanaji Deshmukh and was, in April 1967, sworn in as Chief Minister at the head of the Samyukta Vidhayak Dal (SVD)—a coalition ranging from CPI(M) on the left to BJS on the right, with the Republican Party of India, Swatantra Party, Praja Socialist Party and 22 Independents in between. This was the Jana Sangh's first taste of power. However, Sangh veteran Nanaji Deshmukh subsequently wrote about this experience, 'Our party lost the image of a party with difference. Our people rose as important leaders, but the party of workers was converted into a party of leaders'.

The four years following Charan Singh's rise to power saw four chief ministers and two phases of President's Rule imposed on UP. These years also saw the State's Hindu vote being fractured along caste lines. Charan Singh emerged as the leader of north Indian farmer communities such as Jats, Yadavs, Gujjars, Kurmis and other backward classes, but his government soon ran into rough weather. SVD partner Samyukta Socialist Party (SSP) began an *Angrezi Hatao* (remove English) movement, and two cabinet ministers courted arrest and resigned. Some other parties too withdrew from the coalition and in February 1968, Charan Singh resigned and recommended dissolution of the assembly. A year of central rule followed. Elections were held again in 1969 in which the BKD won 98 seats and Jana Sangh 49. The Congress returned to power with 211 seats in the 425-member House, and Chandra Bhanu Gupta returned as CM. Within a year, however, the Congress split, and Gupta lost majority and resigned. Charan Singh returned as CM in February 1970, this time with the help of Indira Gandhi's Congress (R).

Within months, fresh Congress infighting brought with it a fresh bout of instability. Charan Singh asked for the resignations of 14 ministers belonging to the Congress (R) who, led by Kamlapati Tripathi, refused. Charan Singh recommended the ministers' dismissal, but Governor B Gopala Reddy instead asked Charan Singh to resign. A short spell of President's Rule once again followed after which elections were held. Tribhuvan

Narain Singh was sworn in as Chief Minister at the head of a Samyukta Vidhayak Dal government put together by leaders of the Congress (O), the old guard that was opposed to Indira Gandhi.

Tribhuvan Narain Singh lasted barely five months in the chair—he suffered the ignominy of becoming one of the first chief ministers to lose an assembly bye-election (from Maniram in Gorakhpur, March 1971), and had to resign. Kamlapati Tripathi succeeded him and remained Chief Minister until June 1973, when a revolt by the Provincial Armed Constabulary in demand of better pay and work conditions forced him to bow out.

Back again it was to President's Rule. After a few months of which, a Garhwali Brahmin, Hemwati Nandan Bahuguna, became Chief Minister in November 1973. He resigned in November 1975 following differences with Sanjay Gandhi, and was replaced by another Brahmin from the hills, ND Tiwari from Kumaun, then a Sanjay Gandhi crony.

Came 1975 and the notorious Emergency, at the end of which Lok Sabha elections were held in the country, leading to the rout of the Congress in March 1977. Even Indira Gandhi lost from Rae Bareli to a redoubtable maverick Raj Narain. The period of 1977-80 can be termed as the Janata Party experiment. After the Janata party won the 1977 Lok Sabha election, Morarji Desai's central government sacked Congress State governments, including Tiwari's in UP. In the State assembly elections that took place in June after a spell of President's Rule, the Janata Party won 352 of the 425 seats, but a fight for the chief ministership broke out between the Chandra Shekhar and the Charan Singh-Madhu Limaye factions. As a compromise, Raj Narain floated the name of OBC leader Ram Bachan Yadav, but Limaye pushed the case of the more experienced Ram Naresh Yadav, the MP from Azamgarh. Absent a consensus, finally the MLAs voted for

Ram Naresh Yadav, who went on to win the assembly bye-poll from Nidhauli Kalan in Etah district.

It was during the 1977-80 phase of the Janata experiment that the Jana Sangh, as part of the Janata Party, participated in Ram Naresh Yadav's June 1977-February 1979 government. Kalyan Singh—who would later go on to be UP's Chief Minister in the 1990s and was CM till the day of the demolition of the Babri edifice on 6 December 1992—was health minister and Kesari Nath Tripathi, now Governor of West Bengal, was in charge of institutional finance. A young socialist leader Mulayam Singh Yadav, another future UP CM then in his late 30s, became the cooperatives minister in the Ram Naresh Yadav regime.

Ram Naresh Yadav resigned in the wake of the infamous Narayanpur (Deoria) case of police atrocities, and was succeeded by Banarsi Das, a leader of the Vaishya community, in February 1979. In February 1980, soon after coming back to power, Indira Gandhi sacked the Janata government.

The eight years from 1980-88 saw six chief ministers come and go in UP. This is also the period when the Congress stepped on the slippery road to its eclipse in the State. Following the failure of the Janata Party regime at the centre and its ouster, the Congress swept the 1980 elections, winning 309 seats out of 425. Vishwanath Pratap Singh, the Raja of Manda (Allahabad district), became the Chief Minister. In the coterie around Indira, Singh's star was in the ascendant, just as the importance of another Raja, Dinesh Singh of nearby Kalakankar (Pratapgarh), was declining. VP Singh's government saw several allegations of fake police encounters and major law and order incidents, including the Behmai massacre of 1981, in which 20 Rajputs were massacred by the bandit Phoolan Devi. After dacoits killed his brother, Justice Chandrashekhar Pratap Singh, in 1982, VP Singh quit, to be replaced by Shripati Mishra, a Sultanpur Brahmin.

After a stint of two years, Mishra was removed in August 1984, and ND Tiwari got his second shot at chief ministership. The Congress swept to victory in the election held months after Indira's assassination, though this was entirely because of the sympathy wave generated and nothing to do with Tiwari's leadership. However, Rajiv Gandhi remained true to the Congress culture of clipping the wings of regional leaders. Tiwari was replaced with a Thakur from Gorakhpur, Vir Bahadur Singh within months. Singh was CM from September 1985 to June 1988, when Tiwari returned.

Narayan Dutt Tiwari was fated to be the UP Congress politician who would preside over the political debacle of the Congress in the State. Under him, the Congress suffered a historic defeat in 1989, and has never recovered. If anything, its fortunes in India's electorally most important State have only plummeted headlong. But before that, politics in Uttar Pradesh fell into a churn that would eventually go on to rewrite politics in the rest of India.

Nine November 1989 was the day Hindus congregated in large numbers at Ayodhya in the district of Faizabad to lay the foundation of what Hindu organisations intend to be a grand temple to Shri Rama, at the very spot Hindus believe he was born. Ayodhya has been a bone of contention between Hindus and Muslims ever since a Hindu temple commemorating Rama's birthplace was destroyed in 1528 AD by Mir Baqi, a commander of Mughal invader Babar.

In 1986, the Congress government of Rajiv Gandhi used its majority in Parliament to overturn a Supreme Court judgment directing Muslim men to pay alimony to their divorced wives, a case that went on to attain renown as the Shah Bano case. Rajiv Gandhi was forced to appease obscurantist Muslim elements in his party and for fear of losing the Muslim votebank, forced the Congress into capitulation. The resultant Hindu backlash, which albeit built up slowly, forced the Congress into yet another manoeuvre—it opened the locks of the Shri Ram Janmabhoomi atop which then stood the Babri Masjid, in order to assuage Hindu anger at this shameless capitulation to Muslim obscurantism.

While Hindu jubilation at this victory was quick to surge, the resultant Muslim reaction left the Congress in a cleft stick. While it lost its traditional Muslim vote, for the first time in Uttar Pradesh, the Hindu mood turned against it. As the years and the events rolled on, this shift in the Hindu sentiment proved irrevocable. Hindus viewed the Babri Masjid as a symbol of Islamic conquest and Hindu humiliation and were gradually girding themselves up to remove it. The Bharatiya Janata Party began capitalising on this growing Hindu sentiment, with UP politics changing in ways it had not seen or experienced earlier.

The year 1989 also saw the politics of Mandal and the emergence of Mulayam Singh Yadav. There were two contenders for chief ministership as the Janata Dal, formed in 1988 under the leadership of VP Singh, went into assembly elections. Mulayam Singh Yadav was chosen over Ajit Singh, and formed the government with the BJP's outside support, mirroring the situation at the Centre. However, nationwide campaign for erasing the Babri Masjid was gathering momentum. BJP leader LK Advani took out a *rath yatra* for the stated purpose of building a Ram temple at the site in Ayodhya. Then Bihar Chief Minister Lalu Yadav stopped Advani's Ram Temple Rath in Samastipur in October 1990 and arrested the BJP chief, causing the party to withdraw support from both VP Singh's and Mulayam's governments at the Centre and the state respectively.

VP Singh resigned, and the Congress propped up Chandra Shekhar, who broke away from the Janata Dal; in UP too, Mulayam chose to go with Chandra Shekhar's faction, with outside support from the Congress. Both governments fell after the Congress withdrew support, but in the years that followed,

Mulayam emerged as UP's most pro-Muslim leader, ready to go to any lengths to appease them. He did not hesitate to adopt blatantly anti-Hindu and anti-national stands in his pursuit of the halo of the messiah of the Muslims, his government even firing on Hindu *karsewaks*[3] in Ayodhya and Faizabad in 1990, killing many of them, an action that went to permanently polarise the electorate. After thwarting the Congress at the Centre in the days after the fall of Atal Bihari Vajpayee's second government in 1999, Mulayam also established himself as the most prominent face of anti-Congressism in UP since Charan Singh.

To counter the forces of Mandalism,[4] the BJP projected, in the election of 1991, the OBC Lodh leader Kalyan Singh as its chief ministerial candidate. The party won 221 seats in the 425 member house, forming its government in UP for the first time. Kalyan had an eventful tenure, declaring cheating in school Board examinations a cognisable offence, putting criminals, including four MLAs, behind bars, and sacking a minister for violating his orders.

On 6 December 1992, in what became a red letter day for Hinduism, nearly one lakh Hindus congregated at Ayodhya to demolish the Babri Masjid. After years of suffering Islamic destruction of their places of worship and way of life, Hindus finally felt they had got even. The Kalyan Singh government was dismissed along with governments of other BJP Chief

---

3 Devotees volunteering service to the cause of the temple.

4 The Mandal Commission was established in India on 1 January 1979 by the Janata Party government under Prime Minister Morarji Desai with a mandate to 'identify the socially or educationally backward'. It was headed by Indian parliamentarian B P Mandal. The report of the commission was submitted in December 1980. A decade after the commission gave its report, VP Singh, the Prime Minister at the time, tried to implement its recommendations in 1989. The commission estimated that 52% of the total population (excluding SCs and STs), belonging to 3,743 different castes and communities, were 'backward'. The number of backward castes in Central list of OBCs has now increased to 5,013 (without the figures for most of the Union Territories) in 2006 as per National Commission for Backward Classes.

Ministers Sunderlal Patwa (Madhya Pradesh), Bhairon Singh Shekhawat (Rajasthan) and Shanta Kumar (Himachal). The then Prime Minister was PV Narasimha Rao.

Mulayam Yadav formed the Samajwadi Party in 1992 and entered into a strategic partnership with the Bahujan Samaj Party in the polls the following year. Mulayam's Samajwadi Party and the BSP contested 256 and 164 seats respectively, and won 109 and 67. But the understanding did not last, and the BSP walked out in May 1995, reducing the government to a minority. Bad blood between the partners spilt out in an incident, in which several BSP legislators including their leader Mayawati were reportedly beaten by SP musclemen in a guesthouse.

A fallout of the incident was that the BJP became Mayawati's saviour, and a few days later, handed over a letter to Governor Motilal Vora pledging support if the BSP staked claim to form the government. When Mayawati took oath, she made history—giving Dalits a voice in a State in which they are almost 21% of the population. However, a Hindu vote had by now begun consolidating in Uttar Pradesh, of which the BJP was seen as being the representative. Mulyam Yadav continued to remain the champion of Muslim votes, as the community, fearful of a Hindu consolidation, looked to him to check the BJP. The Congress had by now been squeezed out of any meaningful space in Uttar Pradesh. On the one hand, it was loath to displease the Muslims now captive to Mulayam's politics and on the other, it steadily lost whatever Hindu support it had, which swung to the BJP.

In the 1996 assembly elections, the BJP secured 174 seats, 39 short of a majority. The assembly was kept in suspended animation, following which President's Rule was imposed. Narasimha Rao was still the PM. In April 1997, the BJP entered into an arrangement with the BSP—which had 67 MLAs—under which the parties would have a CM for 2 years by rotation. Mayawati had the first six months, but after making way for Kalyan Singh, she alleged that he had revoked orders issued by her in the interest of Dalits, and withdrew support.

The BJP responded by breaking both the BSP and Congress—a new group called Janatantrik BSP headed by Chaudhary Narendra Singh, and another called Loktantrik Congress led by Naresh Aggrawal lent support to the BJP government headed by Kalyan Singh. In a dramatic incident on 21 February 1998, with Lok Sabha elections in progress, UP Governor Romesh Bhandari dismissed Kalyan Singh's government and swore in Jagdambika Pal of the Congress in his place. Kalyan Singh challenged the dismissal of his government in Allahabad High Court. On the direction of the High Court, he was sworn in again as Chief Minister on 23 February. Pal, a chief minister for no more than 48 hours, is now a Lok Sabha MP of the BJP.

The BJP, despite being a beneficiary of Hindu sentiment and growing anger at the Muslim appeasement by all secular parties, did not stand openly for the Hindu cause. Not surprisingly, the party, which in the 1998 Lok Sabha election had won 58 out of 85 seats in 1999 saw its tally fall to a mere 29. The result of the lobbying against Kalyan Singh saw an octogenarian Ram Prakash Gupta being propelled to chief ministership—party insiders say Kalyan had refused to resign to make way for Rajnath Singh, then the Union Surface Transport Minister.

Kalyan Singh subsequently left the BJP, taking away some of its OBC support. Gupta too didn't last; within months, his detractors in the party started spreading the rumour that he had a flickering memory and would fail to recognise even cabinet colleagues. In the end, Rajnath Singh became CM in October 2000—but the BJP's repeated flip-flops on Hindutva and feet-dragging on the Ram temple issue led to its defeat in 2002. It could win only 88 seats and slipped to third place.

In his 18 months as Chief Minister, Rajnath Singh worked

on a social engineering plan for the BJP. To divide the OBCs, he appointed a committee headed by the current MP from Kairana, Hukum Singh, which recommended that Jats were more backward than Yadavs in the State. He sought the advice of many and made extensive tours of villages to meet farmers. But he could not win UP for the BJP, and came away to Delhi as a party general secretary, and later replaced Ajit Singh as Agriculture Minister in Vajpayee's government.

Following a spell of President's Rule from March to May, 2002, Mayawati became Chief Minister for the third time after the BJP extended support to the BSP. BJP state president Kalraj Mishra resigned, and was replaced by Vinay Katiyar, who conjured up slogans like 'Haathi nahin Ganesh hai, Brahma Vishnu Mahesh hai' to defend the alliance. But problems kept mounting, and Mayawati resigned in August 2003.

On the 29 of that month, Mulayam Yadav was sworn in as Chief Minister with the support of BSP dissidents, and ran a government until 2007. It is said that BJP leaders convinced Vajpayee that Mulayam would help in the 2004 Lok Sabha election which proved a non-event.The NDA, which by then believed more in 'India Shining' and was shy of even mentioning Hindutva, lost power at the Centre. The SP got 39 Lok Sabha seats, its highest ever.

Mayawati's fourth stint as Chief Minister was historic because it rode on the first single-party majority in the Assembly since 1991. Mulayam's 2003-07 government had faced severe criticism for growing crime and bad law and order in the State. Mayawati's social engineering included the Brahmins, whom her mentor Kanshi Ram had opposed tooth and nail, and the Dalit-Brahmin combination brought her 206 out of 403 seats. In 2012, Mayawati became the first CM of UP to complete her full five-year tenure.

Under Mulayam, the SP had developed the reputation of being a party of musclemen. The BJP brought Uma Bharti from

Madhya Pradesh to contest the Charkhari seat in Bundelkhand, but word was out that Mulayam would make his son, the young engineer Akhilesh Yadav, Chief Minister. His promises of free laptops and dole for unemployed youth worked. The SP won 224 of 403 seats, and Akhilesh was sworn in as the youngest chief minister of the State at age 38. Like Mayawati, he completed his five-year term.

In 2017, Uttar Pradesh responded overwhelmingly to Narendra Modi's call by handing the BJP a thumping majority in the State assembly election with 323 seats out of a total of 401. The choice for the chief ministership has been Yogi Adityanath, an ascetic head of the Gorakhnath Temple in Gorakhnath and an adherent of a militant Hindu sect. Adityanath's ascent, underscores the message that Hindutva has now come to occupy the centre stage in India's politics. More importantly, it also conveys to the world at large that Hindus will no longer be apologetic about their identity, which they believe to be the nation's defining ethos.

Uttar Pradesh—A Saga of Jihadi Assault and Hindu Revival

The history of about 1,200 years of Islamic presence in India merits thousands of pages. For the purposes of this book, it is pertinent to highlight here the ravages wrought by Muslim rule on Uttar Pradesh, in the process uncovering important but less known (or perhaps not known at all) events of this period. Also, a honest and factual coverage of the events of this period will demolish the myths spawned by Leftist-Nehruvian (and also some British) historians that Muslim invaders simply walked into India and ruled it unchallenged for over a thousand years until the British in turn conquered it from them. This is contrary to facts, which are presented below.

Most Indian readers, fed on established history books, would be surprised to know that it is the Hindus who resisted the onslaught of Arabs for over twelve centuries unlike the regions west and north of Arabia, which succumbed immediately to Islamisation. It took over 500 years for the Arabs and Turks to lay a foundation for their empire in India and another two centuries before a stable empire could be formed after Akbar's reign (1556-1605 AD). The kingdom Akbar established too perished after a century.

Equally important is that fact that the Arabs did not rule India. Actually, Arab rule anywhere in India was confined to only Sind for only 150 years, and a small kingdom in Mathura for a few years, although many Arab families settled in the country. Muslim rulers were mostly Turks and Afghans. Several Turk families had settled in Afghanistan from where they came into India and their senior officers also included those from Iran.

It should be noted that the Turkish race originated in Central Asia which was mostly a part of the erstwhile Soviet Union. Actually, the Turks were initially imported as slaves, both domestic and military, from beyond the eastern borders of Islam in the ninth century. They gradually rose to high ranks in the military and ultimately took over the Muslim world as its empire builders. From 960 AD onwards entire Turkish tribes were converted; these converts moved to the Middle-East in waves and changed the whole demography of the region including that of the present day Turkey. The Turks accepted Islam without any reservations, sinking their national identity in it and becoming its greatest champions, relegating even the Arabs to the background. Later on, they were joined by another central Asian tribe, the mostly-Buddhist Mongols who had themselves become victims of Islam.

Babasaheb Ambedkar (1891-1956) has stated in his book on Pakistan (*Pakistan or The Partition of India,* Vol. 8, Babasaheb Ambedkar; Reprinted by Education Dept; Govt. of Maharashtra, 1990):

> These invasions of India by Muslims were as much invasions of India as they were wars among the Muslims themselves. This fact has remained hidden, because the invaders are all lumped together as Muslims without distinction. But as a matter of fact, they were Tartars, Afghans and Mongols....

> They were not a loving family cemented by the feeling of Islamic brotherhood. They were deadly rivals of one another and their wars were often wars of mutual extermination. What is, however, important to bear in mind is that with all their internecine conflicts, they were all united by one common objective and that was to destroy the Hindu faith.

It should also be noted that these rulers considered the local converted Muslims as second class Muslims. Aurangzeb (1617-1707; who ruled from 1658-1707), for instance, has often remarked, *'We Turks, you Hindusthanis'* to both Indian Hindus and Muslims. Even in the 'enlightened' Mughal period (mostly from 1526-1707), over seventy per cent of the senior administrative and military posts were in the hands of Muslim foreigners. There are only a few instances of local Indian Muslims establishing kingdoms like the Sultans of Gujarat and the Nizamshahi of Ahmednagar. There is thus no substance to the claim by Indian Muslims that they ruled over India for over a thousand years.

Hindu kingdoms put up a sustained and valorous resistance to the invaders, but despite their valour, could not prevent the Muslim invaders from running over India. One must take into consideration that most accounts of the Muslim period have been written by Muslim and some British historians and are both distorted and exaggerated in their favour.

Many reasons can be given for Muslim successes. The greatest fault lies in Hindus not studying the scriptures and psychology of the invaders, which would have given a clue to their behaviour. Hindus naively expected their ancient standards of *dharmic,* ie. ethical warfare to be reciprocated by the invaders. Whenever Muslim invaders were defeated by Hindus, they were magnanimously pardoned *and allowed to go back. But they used the reprieve only to regroup and attack treacherously again. Hindus never understood this.* It is a lacuna that tragically still persists even to this day.

There is also no basis to Muslim claims as well as secular myths that the British captured power from Muslim rulers or empires. *The most important conquests of the British of the cities of Delhi, Agra, Lahore and Peshawar, and the bulk of the territory were from Marathas, Sikhs and other non-Muslim rulers.* Only Bengal-Bihar, middle and eastern Uttar Pradesh in India were captured from Muslim rulers.

Following Prophet Muhammad's death, Islam's founder (born 570 AD-died 632 AD), his successors the Caliphs, despite internal politicking and bloodletting, expanded Islam's boundaries within the next 10-12 years to cover the territories of the two great powers of the time, the Byzantine and the Sassanid empires. Between 637 and 651 AD Persia was conquered and the Islamic borders touched Afghanistan (Gandhara, ie. today's Kandahar), which was then a part of India. Egypt fell in 641 AD. By 718 AD Spain was conquered. Even Southern France was annexed for a few years. Within one hundred years of the Prophet's death, the Arabs became the masters of a vast region extending from the Bay of Biscay to the Indus and the frontiers of China, and from the Aral Sea to the Upper Nile.

Caliph Umar had sent a naval expedition in 636 AD itself to capture the port of Thane (now a suburb of Mumbai) in India, but the attack was successfully repulsed. Immediately thereafter, the ports of Bharuch in Gujarat and Debal in Sind were unsuccessfully attacked. Umar wanted to avenge these defeats by attacking Makran (Baluchistan), but the Governor of Iran, Abu Musa, realising that it would be futile in view of the strength of the ruler of Sind, Chachrai, advised him that 'He should no more think of Hind (ie. India)'. *It should be noted that this happened at the time when the Arab armies were marching victoriously in the west.* Umar wisely decided to concentrate on expanding his sway over Turkish-speaking territories of Outer Mongolia, Bukhara, Tashqand (Taskent), Samarqand (Samarkand) etc.

During Ali's reign (656–661 AD), his army invaded Sind again under the leadership of General Heras, which advanced up to Kikan where it was routed with severe losses incurred by them. During the Caliphate of Muwahiyah, six expeditions were lead by the Arabs to capture Sind, all of which were beaten back. It was only in 680 AD, after many attempts and a fierce campaign that Makran or Baluchistan (in today's Pakistan, then a part of India) could be subjugated.

In 708 AD, a 4,000-strong Arab army under the command of Budial attacked Deval, only to suffer a rout. A larger well equipped force was sent under Muhammad bin Qasim, which captured Deval by treachery. Sind ruler Dahir proved an easy target. Muhammad captured Sind including Multan after a year in 713 AD, but he had to be recalled and there was again a revival of Hindu power; the Arabs were able to retain only a toehold of land along the coastal strip. In 718 AD, Junaid, the then Governor of Sind again defeated Dahir's son and pressed forward into Gujarat and Kashmir, where he was repelled by Pulakesin and Lalitaditya respectively. Thus the Arabs were again confined only to Sind.

Muslim Thrust into Uttar Pradesh

Subuktigin's son, the infamous Mahmud (of Ghazni), ascended the throne in 998 AD and ruled until his death in AD 1030. He invaded India 17 times between AD 1001 and 1027. He first annexed large territories of Persia and then turned his attention towards India. While his earlier attacks were more for loot and plunder and the powerful Hindu rulers like the remnants of the imperial Magadhan Guptas and Shahis of Afghanistan could contain these, he now wanted to overrun this ancient civilisation with the intention of wiping out Hindus and Hinduism.

Mahmud first attacked Jaipal of Peshawar, only narrowly managing to defeat him. However, Jaipal, unable to stomach his defeat, committed suicide. Jaipal's son Anandpal too met with defeat, but instead of learning any lesson, offered help to Mahmud when the latter was attacked by another Turkish leader, expecting to win Mahmud's lifelong friendship! This was obviously not reciprocated and Mahmud attacked him again in 1008 AD. Anandpal sought the assistance of neighbouring

Hindu rulers. The rival armies camped facing each other for forty days and a bitter battle ensued. Unfortunately, just as the Hindu forces were about to win, the elephant carrying the king was scared with naphtha balls, and when the army saw it fleeing, lost its courage and fled. But Mahmud too had to return back to Ghazni at that time. After Anandpal's death, Mahmud attacked again in 1013 AD and gradually eliminated his successors until 1026 AD. Thus the Shahi kingdom which guarded the borders of India for 1,500 years since 500 BC came to an end.

Mahmud now turned his attention to other territories. He attacked the Chandellas in 1018 AD. When he saw a powerful enemy army facing him, he returned to Ghazni. *The Chandella army at this stage could have decisively finished him, but, as usual, it was another instance of misplaced Hindu generosity.* His desecration of the famous Somnath temple on the western coast in Gujarat, and his raids encouraged other Muslims also to carry out surprise raids, one such raiding party even reached Banaras (Varanasi) in Uttar Pradesh. This could arguably be called the first major jihadi assault on the territory of UP.

The Hindus rose to the challenge. Hindu chiefs got together and decided to repel the invaders. They joined forces and attacked the Muslim army at Kahsala and convincingly defeated it. The Ghaznavids were completely routed in all regions except Multan and Lahore. In June 1033 AD at Bahraich near Lucknow in UP, Salar Masood Ghazni, nephew of Mahmud of Ghazni (son of Mahmud's sister) was slain with his entire army, with not a single Muslim soldier of Masood's army escaping alive. Raja Bhoj who ruled for around 50 years from 1000 to 1050 AD played a big role in Masood's defeat. The tomb of Salar Masood Ghazni is still there in Bahraich, which continues to be venerated by ignorant Hindus by the name of 'Ghazi Baba ki Mazhar'. It was an alliance of about 17 Hindu kings, led by Raja Suhel Dev, who was one of those 17 and who played a big role in this rout and elimination of Salar Masood Ghazni. Suhel Dev's statue, along with that of Raja Bhoj, stand in Bahraich today.

The Hindu destruction of Salar Masood and his Islamic horde kept Islamic invaders away from India for the next century and a half. For the next few decades, Hindus lived in peace but made no effort to eliminate the marauders from the subcontinent. In fact, many Muslim merchants, Sufis and Mullahs settled in various parts of the country and later acted as spies. This glorious episode of Indian history, of the Hindu victory over Salar Masood in 1033 AD has been completely blanked out by Left historians in India.

Meanwhile the Ghoris replaced the Ghaznis in Kabul. Shahabuddin Ghori fortified Multan and attacked Gujarat in 1178 AD but his army was routed by the Solankis, with Ghori being forced to flee the battlefield at Anhilwara. He later captured southern Sind and Lahore. Prithviraj Chauhan ruled Delhi then. Ghori attacked the Bhatinda fort in 1189 AD and captured it because of lax defence. An irate Prithviraj sent a large army to lay a siege in 1191. In the fierce battle that ensued, Shahabuddin's army was completely routed and he had to capitulate. *Prithviraj committed a big mistake by pardoning Ghori despite routing him, instead of doing what was done to Salar Masood in 1033 AD*. For this blunder, not only did Prithviraj Chauhan pay with his own life along with that of a hundred thousand of his soldiers in the Second Battle of Tarain in Uttar Pradesh, but India also suffered massively for many years, with massacre of Hindus and forced conversions and slavery. Thus Delhi fell into the hands of the Muslims.

It can thus be seen that the initial political progress of Islam in the subcontinent was slow and halting. But from 1200 to 1800 AD, ie. six centuries, large parts of India were under their control.

Shahabuddin Ghori (ruled 1192-1206 or so) appointed

Qutbuddin Aibak, his Turkish slave, as his representative in India. In 1197, Kannauj, Jaunpur and Mirzapur (all in today's Uttar Pradesh) came under his control. It was Gujarat that not only resisted but repulsed him and remained independent for another century, until 1298 AD. Then Allauddin Khilji marched towards Bihar and Bengal but the rulers there held on for some time. His army was repulsed from Assam.

The Turks actually took another two centuries to consolidate their hold over all of India. The Mughals, particularly after Akbar's reign (1556-1605 AD), became emperors of India. But this empire collapsed like autumn leaves within a decade or so after Aurangzeb's death in 1707 AD, ie. just a century after Akbar's death.

Shahabuddin Ghori was killed in 1206 AD and his successors proved weak; Qutbuddin Aibak managed to become the Sultan and ruled until 1210 AD. After a brief rule by his son, his son-in-law, Iltutmish seized power and ruled until 1235 AD. The Slave dynasty was followed by Allauddin Khilji, a ruthless jihadi ruler.

Allauddin Khilji died in 1316 AD, after whom his henchman Malik Kafur nominated his son as successor and began a very repressive career, but was himself beheaded shortly afterwards by his numerous enemies. After a period of confusion, one Ghazi Malik Tughlaq of Turkish blood (1320-25 AD) ultimately crowned himself Sultan under the title Ghiyasuddin Tughlaq. His authority was established over Bengal and North Bihar. Uttar Pradesh too was covered under Tughlaq rule.

Rebellions took place all over but were crushed. The Islamic Sultanate covered almost the whole of India except Rajasthan in around 1335 AD. It could, however, last for only about 15 years and it took another 250 years before a full-fledged Mughal empire could be established. But Tughlaq's policy of replacing local Hindu chieftains with Muslim governors enabled the establishment of many local Muslim kingdoms and hence Muslims effectively ruled a large portion of India during this period. The Sultan was succeeded by his cousin, Firoz Shah (1351-88 AD). He was an iconoclast and destroyed many temples. He was followed by a number of successors from his family.

The end of the Tughlaqs brought about a period of great confusion. The Sayyads were the next to rule regions around Delhi between 1414 and 1451 AD. They were not very competent and their rule extended only to regions around Delhi. They were succeeded by the Afghani Lodis (1451-1526 AD). Bahlol was the first Lodi ruler who reconquered the neighboring territories so that his rule extended from the Punjab to the western frontiers of Bihar. His son Sikandar (1489-1517 AD) extended it to Bihar and Bengal. He shifted his capital to Agra. He desecrated the shrines in Mathura and constantly humiliated the Hindus. After his death, Ibrahim ascended the throne after killing his brother. He treated his nobles so badly that they, chiefly his brother Daulat Khan Lodi who was the Subedar of Punjab, invited Babar, the then king of Kabul and Kandahar, and a descendent of Chengiz Khan and Timur to come to Delhi. Babar had already attempted unsuccessfully to penetrate India. But now he descended afresh and in the first Battle of Panipat in 1526 AD defeated and overthrew Ibrahim Lodi to become the ruler. This was a new epoch in Indian history. Thus, during this period between 1206 and 1526, AD there were as many as 28 rulers from numerous dynasties.

Throughout this sordid saga of Islamic rule, the region of what comprises today's Uttar Pradesh was subject to brutal jihadi rule, pillage, rape, forced conversions and massacres.

The first recorded instance of mass slaughter of Hindus in Uttar Pradesh could be said to be Mohammad Ghori's raid on the region in 1194, following his victory over Prithviraj

Chauhan in the Second Battle of Tarain in 1192. He attacked Varanasi, the holiest of Hindu pilgrimage sites at the end of the 12th century. Ghori continued the destruction of Hindu temples and idols that had begun during the first attack in 1194 (Elliot, Henry Miers 1953, *The History of India: A told by its Own Historians–The Muhammadan period;* Excerpt from *Jamiu'l-Hikayat,* University of Michigan). In another contemporary record, the *Taj-ul-Ma'asir* by Hassn Nizam-i-Naishapuri, it is stated that when Qutb-ud-Din Aibak (of Turko-Afghan origin and the First Sultan of Delhi 1194-1210 AD) conquered Meerut, he demolished all the Hindu temples of the city and erected mosques on their sites. In the city of Aligarh, he converted Hindu inhabitants to Islam by the sword and beheaded all those who adhered to their own religion.

Religious violence in India continued during the reign of Jalaluddin Firoz Shah Khilji and Allauddin Khilji of the Khilji dynasty. Their army commanders such as Ulugh Khan, Nusrat Khan, Khusro Khan and Malik Kafur attacked, killed, looted and enslaved non-Muslim people from North, West, Central and South India. Riots and mutinies by Hindus erupted in various parts of the Sultanate, ranging from modern Punjab to Gujarat to Madhya Pradesh to Uttar Pradesh. These riots were crushed with mass executions, where all men and even boys above the age of eight were seized and killed (Elliot and Dowson, *The History of India: As told by its Own Historians – The Muhammadan Period;* Vol. 3, Trubner & Co, London, pages 164-165, 104-107).

The next major recorded mass slaughter of Hindus in Uttar Pradesh was the execution of slaves by Timur Lang, the Turkish invader from Samarkand. Timur attacked and sacked Delhi in 1398. However, before the battle of Delhi commenced, Timur ordered his soldiers to kill all the 100,000 slaves caught to avoid a rebellion. This slaughter happened at Loni, near today's Ghaziabad in west Uttar Pradesh bordering

Delhi. After the sack of Delhi, the Timurid horde massacred all Hindu inhabitants of Meerut.

After the massacre by Timur, the people and lands within Delhi Sultanate were left in a state of anarchy, chaos and pestilence. Though there are fewer historical records of jihadi massacres by the Sayyid dynasty that followed, the few available records, including the *Tarikh-i Mubarak-Shahi* describe continued religious violence. From 1414 through 1423, according to the Muslim historian Yahya bin Ahmad, the Islamic commanders 'chastised and plundered the infidels' of Ahar, Khur, Kampila, Gwalior, Seori, Chandawar, Etawa, Sirhind, Bail, Katehr and Rahtors. Of these, Etawa falls in modern Uttar Pradesh (Elliot and Dowson, *The History of India: As told by its Own Historians–The Muhammadan Period;* Vol. 3, Trubner & Co, London, pages 47-59).The violence was not one-sided, though; Hindus retaliated by forming their own armed groups, and attacking forts seized by Muslims. In 1431, Jalandhar for example, was retaken by Hindus and all Muslims inside the fort were made prisoner. Yahya bin Ahmad, the historian, remarked on Muslims being taken captive by Hindus, 'the unclean ruthless infidels had no respect for the Musulman religion'.

Muhammad Tughlaq's empire of AD 1335 covered almost all of India barring Rajasthan, but just in 1336 AD, the great Vijaynagar kingdom was founded, which liberated a large part of South India. Actually, during the time of King Krishnadevaraya who ruled from AD 1509-1529, the kingdom extended from Cuttack in the east to Goa in the west and from Raichur Doab in the north to the Indian Ocean in the south. In the map of India in AD 1525 on the eve of Babar's invasion, a far lesser part of India was ruled by Delhi's Muslim rulers—as compared to that under Tughlaq in 1335 AD, with Hindus reconquering a large part of India.

Religious violence and persecution continued during the

reign of the two significant Lodi dynasty rulers, Bahlul Khan Lodi and Sikandar Lodi. The Delhi Sultanate, whose reach had shrunk to northern and eastern India, witnessed burning and killing of Hindus on account of their faith in Bengal, Bihar and Uttar Pradesh. In Uttar Pradesh, a historian of Lodi dynasty times, described the state-sponsored religious violence as follows (this form of religious violence is summarised by multiple Muslim historians, for example in *Zubdatu-t Tawarikh;* Elliot and Dowson, *Zubdatu-i-Tawarikh; The History of India: As Told by Its Own Historians – The Muhammadan Period;* Vol. 6, Trubner & Co., London, page 187):

> He (Lodi) was so zealous a Musulman that he utterly destroyed diverse places of worship of the infidels. He entirely ruined the shrines of Mathura, the minefield of heathenism. Their stone images were given to the butchers to use them as meat weights (Ahmad Yadgar, *Wakiat-i Mushtaki* and other texts describe that this use of stone idol parts to weigh food and particularly meat served as a daily reminder and humiliated the religious sentiments of Hindus who held all killing of animal life to be wrong and practiced vegetarianism) and all the Hindus in Mathura were strictly prohibited from shaving their heads and beards, and performing ablutions. He stopped the idolatrous rites of the infidels there. Every city thus conformed as he desired to the customs of Islam (Táríkh-i Dáúdí, Elliot and Dowson, *History of India: As Told by Its Own Historians–The Muhammadan Period;* Vol. 4, Trubner & Co., London, page 447).

The end of the Delhi Muslim Sultanate dynasties was also the coming of the Mughals. While Babar, Humayun, Akbar, Jahangir and Shah Jahan were all iconoclasts in varying degrees, the most odious of Mughal rulers was Aurangzeb, whose rule saw Mughal barbarism touch new heights. Prayag, called Teerthraj, or foremost among places of pilgrimage for all Hindus, was forcibly renamed Allahabad by Akbar (reign: 1556-1605). The holiest of Hindu temples at Kashi (Varanasi) and Mathura were destroyed to be replaced with mosques in Aurangzeb's time. Historian Mathew White claims an estimated 4.6 million people were killed under his reign. (Matthew White 2011, Aurangzeb in *Atrocities: The 100 Deadliest Episodes in Human History*, WW Norton & Co.) Aurangzeb banned Diwali, re-introduced the *jaziya* (tax) on non-Muslims (Vincent Smith 1919, *The Oxford History of India,* Oxford University Press, page 438). He led numerous campaigns of attacks against non-Muslims, forcibly converted Hindus to Islam and destroyed Hindu temples (Ayalon 1986; p. 271 and Abraham Eraly 2000, *Emperors of the Peacock Throne: The Saga of the Great Mughals;* Penguin Books, pp 398-399).

Babar, after defeating local Muslim chieftains and Rajputs, notably Rana Sanga of Chittor, had to return to Kabul to quell rebellions there, where he died in 1530. Before that however, in 1528, his lieutenant Mir Baqi led an expedition to Ayodhya and desecrated the Shri Ram Janmabhoomi Temple, which all Hindus hold sacred as the birthplace of Shri Ram. Mir Baqi constructed a mosque atop the birthplace, outraging Hindu sentiment, which became infamous as the Babri Masjid. Since then, *Hindus waged 76 battles over a period of 450 years, to reclaim Ayodhya.* The 77th battle culminating in a Hindu victory—was on 6 December 1992, when close to a million Hindus gathered at Ayodhya to bring down the edifice of the Babri Masjid, liberating the Ram Janmabhoomi.

Babar's son, Humayun, succeeded him and continued the wars with local rulers. Humayun was defeated by Sher Shah, a local Afghan, who forced him into exile in Kabul in 1540 AD. Sher Shah ruled northern India from Punjab to Bengal. He was a bigoted ruler and ruthlessly destroyed Hindu kingdoms and temples in north and central India. Humayun recaptured Lahore in 1555 but died in 1556.

Humayun's son, Akbar, succeeded him, by winning the second battle of Panipat in 1556 against Hemu, a Hindu general of Afghan ruler Islam Shah. Hemu alias Hemachandra is a great and forgotten Hindu hero. He was the first Hindu after Prithviraj Chauhan to sit on the throne of Delhi, albeit for a short period of one month—from 7 October 1556 when he was coronated under the title 'Raja Vikramaditya' before the Second Battle of Panipat on 5th November 1556. Born a commoner in a Bania family, Hemu rose to become the Emperor of India, proclaiming Independence from Sher Shah's descendant Shah Adali (who was the ruler till the time Humayun came back to India). *The fact that Hemu proclaimed independence from Shah Adali and had himself coronated under the title Raja Vikramaditya has been suppressed by many historians, who have tried to project him as a perennial general of Shah Adali, which he was not.* Hemu was no fluke ruler or victor. He won 22 successive battles and defeated the Mughals many times, but unfortunately died in the only battle that he lost in his life. Had an arrow not pierced his eye, he would have defeated the Mughals in the Second Battle of Panipat and in all likelihood founded a ruling Hindu dynasty in Delhi, thus liberating Hindus from oppression.

Akbar now became the undisputed ruler. He made a significant move by befriending the Rajputs who were appointed by him to high positions. Thus, his sway also extended to Rajasthan which had mostly escaped the Muslim rule so far. Only the famous Rana Pratap refused to succumb, and went on to symbolise undying Hindu resistance. Despite repeated attempts, the Mughal Empire failed to defeat or subdue Rana Pratap.

After Akbar's death in AD 1605, his son Salim ruled under the title 'Jahangir' from 1605 to 1627. Jahangir died in 1627 to be succeeded by his son Khurram or Shah Jahan who ruled from 1627 to 1657. Immediately on accession, Shah Jahan had to face rebellion from the Bundelas. They were conquered by his son Aurangzeb who treated the Hindu prisoners with terrible inhumanity typical of him. The Bundelas were not completely subdued and later Raja Chhatrasal (1649-1731) challenged the authority of the Mughals in Bundelkhand, which consisted parts of today's Uttar Pradesh and Madhya Pradesh. When he was just 22, Chhatrasal met the great Shivaji in 1671 and expressed his desire to serve under the Hindu monarch. Shivaji advised him to establish his own kingdom.

In 1657 Shah Jahan fell ill and the usual blood-soaked process of succession commenced amongst his sons. The eldest, Prince Dara, a poet and an admirer of Hindu scriptures, had earlier been appointed successor but the crafty Aurangzeb eliminated his brothers one by one, put his father in prison and became emperor in 1658 and until his death in 1707 and for fifty long years proved to be an unmitigated curse on the Hindus. Temple destruction and conversion were rampant, with the Hindus of Uttar Pradesh suffering enormously. The Keshav Rai temple at Mathura and Kashi Vishwanath temple were destroyed by Aurangzeb during his reign.

It was only after the advent of the Marathas under Shivaji that Hindu rule was finally reestablished. The great Shivaji was born in 1627 and, inspired by his mother and tutor, steadily and astutely built up his kingdom by simultaneously tackling hostile powers like the Mughals, and the Adilshahi and Nizamshahi rulers. By the time he died in 1680 he had laid the firm foundation for a Hindu empire. His son, Sambhaji, unparalleled in valour and given the title *Dharmaveer* (hero of the faith), preferred a very torturous death rather than converting to Islam.

After Shivaji's death in 1680, Sambhaji faced simultaneous opposition of the mighty Aurangzeb, Adilshah, Nizamshah, the Portuguese of Goa and the Siddis (a Muslim tribe of Abyssinian descent). But he stoutly fought and defended his kingdom for almost nine years, till his treacherous capture and horrific torture to death on 11 March 1689 by Aurangzeb. The mighty Mughal personally came down to the south in 1682 after Shivaji's death to vanquish the Marathas and other rulers and extend the Mughal empire all over India. But the Marathas would prove to be his nemesis. *Aurangzeb, who had crossed the Narmada and the Vindhyas, could never return to the north. Unflinching Maratha resolve and their unrelenting counter-attacks on him not only bogged him down, eventually compelling him to admit defeat, but also buried him and his Mughal Empire in the Deccan forever.* The Marathas then went on to rule virtually all of India, from Attock (in today's Balochistan) to Cuttak and even parts of Bengal. The end of Mughal rule and Maratha domination of nearly all of India brought relief for Hindus, including those in Uttar Pradesh. Maratha rulers restored many Hindu temples over north India, including those in UP. (The Marathas ruled Delhi de-facto after 1761 till at least 1794; Bajirao I had captured Delhi in AD 1737 as well, though there was a nominal Mughal puppet on the throne.)

Maratha rule was replaced by the British towards the latter part of the 18th century and by the earlier part of the 19th century, it was the British who were gradually gaining ascendancy over India. *Muslims, never reconciled to the loss of their status as rulers and forced to reckon with first a Hindu resurgence and then advancing British rule, made a strange common cause with Hindus in the Mutiny of 1857 against the British, but this was no Hindu-Muslim common front against the European power.* Rather, it was the coming together of disgruntled elements against a common foe. Muslims sought to resurrect their fallen rule. Indeed, even as the campaign of the mutineers of 1857 against the East India Company wore on, there were ample incidents in western UP, of Muslims turning on Hindus. For them, jihad was primarily against the Hindu and only incidentally against the Englishman. In a particularly telling incident, the Muslims in Muazzampur Narayan, in the district of Bijnor in western UP lost no time in turning upon their Hindu neighbours as soon as the mutineers had driven out the small British garrison during the 1857 uprising. For them, the departure of the British meant a return to Mughal rule; ie. targeting the Hindus.

Following the failure of the 1857 Mutiny and the firm ensconcing of British rule in India, Muslims became even more obscurantist, as they were unable to come to terms with the winds of modernity sweeping India. English education and jobs were the new order of the day, slowly obliterating the old feudal world of the Islamic sultanates. Hindus, by and large, were quick to recognise the changing world and took to English education. Gradually, intellectual and economic control of India's life shifted from Muslim to Hindu hands. Never a productive or entrepreneurial people, Muslims now began to sense their socio-economic backwardness accentuated by the loss of political power even more. This was more acutely felt by Muslims in Delhi and Uttar Pradesh. The British too, at that time, saw an Islamic hand behind the Mutiny. It was not a surprise therefore that the Muslim mind began yearning for a past that was impossible to restore. The outcome soon manifested itself in growing Muslim communalism.

Syed Ahmad bin Muttaqi Khan or Syed Ahmad Khan, (17th October 1817-27th March 1898), commonly known as Sir Syed, was a Muslim leader and educationist of nineteenth century British India. Born into a family with strong ties with the now-deceased Mughal court, Syed studied the Quran and sciences within the court and later law from the University of Edinburgh.

Sir Syed was personally affected by the violence and the ending of the Mughal dynasty amongst many other long-standing kingdoms. Sir Syed and many other Muslims took this as a defeat of Muslim society. He supported the British during the 1857 uprising. In 1859 Sir Syed published the booklet *Asbab-e-Baghawat-e-Hind* (The Causes of the Indian Revolt) in which he delineated the causes of the Indian revolt. In this, his most famous work, he rejected the common notion that the conspiracy was planned by Muslim élites, who were insecure at the diminishing influence of Muslim monarchs. He now wanted Muslims to be loyal to the British Empire and believed that his community could not progress without Western education and science.

He went on to establish the Mohammedan Anglo-Oriental College in Aligarh in 1875, which later morphed into the Aligarh Muslim University (AMU) in 1920. *In later years, Aligarh and its Muslim University would serve as the arsenal of the movement for a separate Pakistan.* Sir Syed was also opposed to the promotion of Hindi and wanted Muslims to fiercely adhere to Urdu as their lingua franca. The growth of Hindi in Syed's eyes was further proof of the erosion of centuries-long Islamic domination and of Hindu resurgence. Testifying before a British-appointed education commission, Sir Syed controversially exclaimed that 'Urdu was the language of the gentry and Hindi that of the vulgar'. His remarks provoked a hostile response from Hindu leaders, who unified across the nation to demand the recognition of Hindi.

It was the early manifestation of the two-nation Theory, of which Syed Ahmad Khan was an early and ardent proponent; he said—first at Lucknow in 1887 and then at Meerut in 1888—that Hindus and Muslims are two separate nations. While fearful of the loss of Muslim political power owing to the community's backwardness, Sir Syed was also averse to the prospect of democracy, which would give control of government to the Hindu majority. Said he: 'At this time our nation is in a bad state in regards education and wealth, but God has given us the light of religion and the Quran is present for our guidance, which has ordained them (the British) and us to be friends. Now God has made them rulers over us. Therefore we should cultivate friendship with them, and should adopt that method by which their rule may remain permanent and firm in India, and may not pass into the hands of the Bengalis (Hindus; when Syed said this, many prominent Indian leaders were from Bengal). If we join the political movement of the Bengalis our nation will reap a loss, for we do not want to become subjects of the Hindus instead of the subjects of the "people of the Book"'. *It was Sir Syed who played an active role in the formation of the Muslim League. Syed Ahmad is regarded in Pakistan as one of the founding fathers of its creation.*

Uttar Pradesh is also the birthplace of a prominent Islamic obscurantist movement—the Deobandi movement. *Deobandi is a revivalist movement within Sunni (primarily Hanafi) Islam.* It is centered in India, Pakistan, Afghanistan and Bangladesh, and has recently spread to the United Kingdom, and has a presence in South Africa. The name derives from the town Deoband, Uttar Pradesh, about 150 kilometres from Delhi. It is here that the Islamic seminary and school Darul Uloom Deoband is situated. *The movement was inspired by scholar Shah Waliullah Dehlawi (1703–1762), who was witness to the loss of Mughal power and its descent into subordination to the victorious Marathas, who entered Delhi in 1737 and reduced the then Mughal emperor Shah Alam to the status of a protected vassal.* The Deobandi movement was founded in 1867 in the wake of the failed Sepoy Mutiny a decade earlier. Although the Deobandis had, on paper, opposed Partition, this had nothing to do with any patriotic sentiment. The Deobandi School stands for complete Islamisation of India.

The Darul Uloom has a major role in the increasing radicalisation of Muslims, also issuing *fatwas* (religious edicts) from time to time on just about any issue. In January 2012, scholars from a Deobandi school issued a fatwa calling for the author Salman Rushdie to be barred from entering India to attend a literature festival because he had offended Muslim sentiments by his novel *The Satanic Verses,* which also earned him a death threat by then Iranian religious ruler Ayatollah Khomeini in 1989. In May 2010, clerics from a Deobandi school issued a fatwa stating that men and women cannot work together in public offices unless the women are properly clothed. In September 2013, scholars from a Deobandi school issued a fatwa banning photography as un-Islamic. *Deoband, in fact, can rightly be said to the precursor of the Aligarh Muslim University. The Deoband school might not have supported Partition, but it is its teaching that produced the Taliban in Afghanistan and Pakistan.* After Pakistan's humiliating defeat to India in 1971, its breakup and the birth of Bangladesh, Deobandi theologians reportedly advised Pakistani dictator Zia-ul-Haq after 1977 to opt for covert warfare against India, as open warfare for Pakistan against its bigger and more powerful Hindu adversary (India) was not militarily possible. The results of this Deobandi teaching are now apparent in the form of Islamic terrorism against India, which have now spread to other major regions of the world. *It would indeed be apt to call the Islamic terror outfit, the Islamic State of Iraq and Syria (ISIS), the West Asian products of the Deobandi school of thought.*

Come the 20th century, and Muslim communalism only worsened in UP, then known as United Provinces, and elsewhere in India. The Indian national Congress had been formed in 1885 and after the advent of Mohandas Karamchand Gandhi, appeasing Muslims at any cost became the party's credo. *Gandhi's first major dabbling in Muslim politics was his atrocious and ill-fated support to the Khilafat movement, which Muslims in India and elsewhere waged for the reinstatement of the Caliph of Turkey.* Turkey's Ottoman Sultan had ruled as the Caliph of all Muslims until that country's defeat in the First

World War, that led to the collapse and end of the 800-year-old Ottoman Sultanate. The Khilafat movement (1919–22) was a pan-Islamic, political protest campaign launched by Muslims of the British Empire to influence the British government not to abolish the Ottoman Caliphate. The movement occurred simultaneously with the Noncooperation Movement of 1921. The stated objective of the movement, according to Gandhi and the Congress, was increasing Hindu-Muslim unity. However, Mustafa Kemal Attaturk, a modern and secular Turk, seized power and abolished the institution of the Caliphate in 1924, which was seen as an affront by Muslims the world over. Turkish Muslims, however, welcomed Attaturk's progressive reforms.

In India, the Khilafat movement was an unmitigated disaster. Its dream of resurrecting the Ottoman Caliphate was of course an impossibility, but in India, far from achieving any Hindu-Muslim unity, it only stoked Muslim belligerence towards Hindus and led to the most murderous riots seen in India for a long time, the most horrific of which was the Moplah jihadi riots on Hindus in Kerala in 1921. The movement collapsed by late 1922, but not before leaving a trail of blood due to Muslim rioting. The Khilafat movement also strengthened the Aligarh school of separatist thought. No wonder, scholars like Husein Khimjee would later call Pakistan a legacy of the Khilafat movement.

Provincial elections were held in British India in January 1946 to elect members of the legislative councils of British Indian provinces. The elections laid the foundation for the creation of Pakistan. The Muslim League finished second, but it had won the overwhelming majority of Muslim seats. It won nearly one-third of India, and as such, gained the negotiating power to begin partitioning India. This was done as it became evident that a united India would be politically unstable. In UP, the League won 54 out of 228 seats. More tellingly, a group of students of the Aligarh Muslim University went to the Punjab to campaign for the League, and also to canvass support for the creation of Pakistan. When told by their co-religionists in Punjab that Pakistan would come into being on India's northwest and therefore, not be of much benefit to UP, the AMU campaigners replied that even if that were so, they would feel happy as their ummah (worldwide Muslim community) had achieved their cherished dream of a separate Muslim country!

The violence that followed the 1947 partition of India scarred Uttar Pradesh as well, though there was no major outbreak of communal violence in the State for the next couple of decades. But at the end of the 1970s and early '80s, Muslim separatism began rearing its sinister head. Serious communal riots took place in Meerut in 1982 and 1987. From 1986 onwards, Muslims also began going on the warpath because of Hindu assertiveness over the Ram Janmabhoomi issue. Hindus had been enraged over endless appeasement of the Muslim community, a feeling that reached a boiling point over the Shah Bano issue that year, in which the Congress showed no qualms in overturning even a Supreme Court judgment granting alimony rights to a divorced Muslim widow. Pent-up Hindu resentment burst forth on 6th December 1992, sending the Babri mosque in Ayodhya crashing to dust. Riots in the country and in Uttar Pradesh followed.

The BJP benefited from this Hindu assertiveness and rode to power in UP, first in 1991 before the Babri demolition and then in 1997, but did nothing to fulfil its promises to the Hindus, leading to the community's disenchantment with the party. It lost power towards the end of the decade of the '90s, to be replaced by blatantly casteist parties like the Samajwadi Party and Bahujan Samaj Party, under whom appeasement of Muslims touched dangerous heights, with openly anti-India jihadi elements being coopted into the State's power apparatus.

A steady groundswell of Hindu nationalist sentiment built up over the first decade of the 2000s, but could not be translated into political power owing to the lack of any tall Hindu leader at either the State or the centre. The years 2014, and later 2017 in Uttar Pradesh have turned out to be epochs, with Hindus firmly uniting behind Narendra Modi and delivering an unambiguous message—it is they who will write India's destiny.

Ghazni to Alamgir

'The richly jewelled idols taken from the pagan temples were transferred to Agra and there placed beneath the steps leading to the Nawab Begum Sahib's mosque, in order that they might ever be pressed under foot by the true believers. The city's name was changed to Islamabad.' Can you guess the name of this unfortunate place? We can tell you who published those words. He was Vincent A Smith ICE, CIE, the famous historian. The account is of the repeated destruction by Islamic invaders.

If you cannot guess, it was Mathura, the birthplace of Shri Krishna. Most of the idols were from the destroyed Kesava Deva Mandir, built at the spot where the popular avatar was believed to have incarnated some 3,400 years ago. If Mahmud of Ghazni was a *jaahil* or a barbarian, one might have been inclined to overlook his outrage and excuse him. But both Al Barooni and Utbi, who were chroniclers and lived in Ghazni's times, certified that Mahmud was devout and built beautiful mosques in his Ghazni. For this author, it is difficult to do unto others what he would dislike others doing unto him. It is not easy for a conscience to live with double standards. The author is not a regular worshipper and yet he can appreciate what *puja*, prayer or *ibadat* means to others. He would hate to disturb them. This is in the domain of sentiment. Beyond that, of course, is the Hindu in him which tells him that every *karma* leads to *bhagya*, every deed goes to shape destiny. Every action has a reaction, equal and opposite.

This reasoning must have been alien to Mahmud of Ghazni in 1017 AD, although his forefathers must have been Hindu or Buddhist, or possibly, pagan (there was no Islam until the 7th century). Viewed thus, the misfortunes of the Afghan people, especially since the Soviet invasion in April 1978 are the bhagya resulting from the karmas of iconoclasts like Mahmud. He was not the only bloodthirsty invader. There were a series of them from Afghanistan. The last big vandal was Ahmed Shah Abdali of the 18th century. What was perpetrated at Mathura is unthinkable in any context of civilisation.

You will experience it better when you read what a British Christian had to say. As a Hindu, all that I can say is that no one is more widely adored amongst us than Shri Krishna. From Jammu in the north to Kanyakumari in the south, from Dwarka in the west to Imphal in the east, there are any number of Krishna worshippers. Moreover, there is no Hindu who would not be an adorer of this son of Mathura. He is believed to have given the *Bhagvad Gita* to us. Even today, every Hindu swears by it before answering in any court, just as Christians and Muslims swear by the Bible and the Quran respectively. If there be any one book from which a Hindu wishes to understand his faith, it is the *Gita.* In fact, everyone, at least in India, understands what Krishna means to the Hindu psyche. Just as Rama exemplifies the uncompromising idealist, Krishna personifies the comprehensive realist. When a Hindu has a problem, he wonders what Kesava would have done to solve it with his genius for tactics and strategy. If he wishes to celebrate a festival, he thinks of Giridhar Gopal. If he dreams of frolic, he sees Gopinath. If he looks for love, he cannot but help dream of Radheshyam.

In his *Mathura: A District Memoir*, Collector FS Growse (first published in 1874) has recorded his exhaustive survey and research about Brajbhoomi. He was so overwhelmed by the vandalism that visited the area repeatedly, that he wrote feelingly, although his home was in far away England. To quote: 'Thanks to Muhammadan intolerance, there is not a single building of any antiquity either in the city itself or its environs. Its most famous temple—that dedicated to Kesava Deva (Krishna)—was destroyed in 1669, the eleventh year of the reign of the iconoclast Aurangzeb (Alamgir was also his name). The mosque (idgah) erected on its ruins is a building of little architectural value.'

Mahmud of Ghazni was the first iconoclast to vandalise Mathura. That was in 1017 AD about which Growse wrote:

> If anyone wished to construct a building equal to the Kesava temple existing then he would not be able to do so without expending a hundred million dinars, and the work would occupy two hundred years, even though the most able and experienced workmen were employed. Orders were given that all the temples should be burnt with naphtha and fire and levelled with the ground. The city was given up to plunder for twenty days. Among the spoils are said to have been five great idols of pure gold with eyes of rubies and adornments of other precious stones, together with a vast number of smaller silver images, which, when broken up, formed a load for more than a hundred camels. The total value of the spoils has been estimated at three millions of rupees; while the number of Hindus carried away into captivity exceeded 5,000.

Today Balkrishna is worshipped in a little room which

appears like a servant's quarter at the bottom of the *idgaah*. Pathos can be experienced by any visitor, whether a devotee or otherwise. To go back to Aurangzeb, over two centuries after the desecration, Growse felt that: 'Of all the sacred places in India, none enjoys a greater popularity than the capital of Braj, the holy city of Mathura. For nine months in the year, festival follows upon festival in rapid succession and the ghats and temples are daily thronged with new troops of way-worn pilgrims. So great is the sanctity of the spot that its panegyrists do not hesitate to declare that a single day spent at Mathura is more meritorious than a lifetime passed at Banaras. All this celebration is due to the fact of it being the birthplace of the demigod Krishna.'

In his chapter entitled 'The Braj Mandai, the Ban Yatra and the Holi' Growse writes: 'Not only the city of Mathura, but with it, the whole of the western half of the district has a special interest of its own as the birthplace and abiding home of Vaishnava Hinduism. It is about 42 miles in length with an average breadth of 30 miles and is intersected throughout by the river Jamuna. In the neighbourhood is Gokul and Brindaban, where the divine brothers Krishna and Balaram grazed their herds.' He continues: 'Almost every spot is traditionally connected with some event in the life of Krishna or of his mythical mistress Radha.'

To paraphrase William Shakespeare, not all the scents of Arabia would suffice to wash away the sins of Ghazni and Alamgir at Mathura. Since it is not possible to claim back what was destroyed long ago, the return of the *idgaah* and the *shuddhi* of Krishna Janmabhoomi or the birthplace of Krishna, is the only alternative.

Qutbuddin and 27 Mandirs

Reporting on the monuments of Delhi in 1871 AD, JD Beglar of the Archaeological Survey of India, had an interesting theory after he explored the Quwwatul Islam mosque which is situated next to the Qutb Minar, ASI Report 1871172. In his words: 'It remains only to add a suggestion that the unsightly layer of irregular stones that cover up the courtyard be removed; it will then be possible to state definitely whether or not a central grand temple existed. From examples elsewhere, I am sanguine that traces of a central shrine will be found on careful examination.'

The legendary world traveller Ibn Batuta was categorical about the mosque being a conversion from a cluster of temples. On the site of the mosque, he wrote, there was a *butkhana* or a house of idols. After the conquest of Delhi, it was turned into a mosque. Even today one cannot fail to notice the image of Ganesh on the rear plinth of the mosque.

Proximity induces apathy, rather like familiarity breeding contempt! Countless people visit Qutb Minar each year. But how many of them remember having seen the mosque next door in Mehrauli, Quwwatul Islam? The story of this mosque is told on the tablet displayed on the spot by the Archaeological Survey of India. It is a story of how 27 temples were desecrated and how their rubble was used to build a mosque in their place. It was to announce to the regional populace that the Raja was gone and the Sultan had taken over.

The desecration had its vicarious side. For, there is no record or mention anywhere that the idol of the presiding deity of the mandir was removed and handed over to the priest for taking away to another temple. In fact, in many cases, there were gleeful references to how the idol was destroyed and its broken pieces were buried under the entrance of the mosque, so that they would be routinely stepped on by those who came visiting for their ibadat.

Ghori evidently had a killer instinct, so lauded in the West as necessary for victory. To kill or not to kill is the privilege of the victor. But monumental humiliation cannot be the doing of anyone except a coward. The desecration of the Mehrauli temples was probably first perpetrated by Mohammad Ghori. It is situated next to the famous Qutb Minar, which originally was a *Visnudhwaja*.

The mosque was located at the citadel which came to be known as Qila Rai Pithora. The conversion began soon after the second Battle of Tarain, in 1192 AD, wherein Mohammad Ghori defeated and killed Prithviraj Chauhan. It might be recalled that in the first battle of Tarain, it was Prithviraj who had defeated Ghori and did not kill him, but let him go. *Kshama veerasya bhushanam* or 'forgiveness is the ornament of a hero' is what the then ruler of Delhi must have had in mind.

The mosque was later named after its builder, Qutbuddin Aibak, as Quwwatul Islam. The name itself is arrogant; for a place of worship, even more so.

Let us quote the version given in the *Oxford History of Islam*: 'The immense congregational mosque in Delhi known as

Quwwat ai-Islam (Might of Islam) was one of the first built in India. Begun in 1191, the mosque stands on the site of a pre-Islamic temple whose ruins were incorporated in the structure. The tall iron pillar in the courtyard, originally dedicated to the Indian god Vishnu around 400 AD, was re-erected as a trophy to symbolise Islam's triumph over Hinduism.'

In those days, there were no means of communication other than the beating of drums which could not reach very far beyond a village. On the other hand, a popular temple was a place of pilgrimage, several times a year. The devotees would suddenly discover that the sanctum of their beloved avatar had been broken into pieces and rebuilt with something that, in their eyes, was devastatingly offensive. Most often the old stones and statues that earlier adorned the temple walls could be recognised. For, they had been used in building the mosque.

The Quwwatul mosque was converted from 27 Hindu and Jain temples that were destroyed. It is a monument to a people's humiliation. If it were not so, all the statuettes that still adorn the pillars in the mosque need not have been so blatantly displayed. Even after 800 years, they are, as it were, alive for the conquered to see. And not only for the conquered but for all their successors who would ever visit this mosque. Surely, it is un-Islamic to have anything to do with images. Portraits and statues are *haraam* and yet Quwwatul Islam has displayed them. If Aibak had been even slightly considerate, not just towards the conquered, but even towards his own religion, he would have covered the figurines with lime and sand.

However, when one reads what Sir Syed Ahmed Khan of Aligarh fame proudly wrote about the destruction of 27 temples, one's impression of Islam gets shaken. What he wrote is best read in his original words (from his Urdu book, *Asar-us-Sanadid*, translated by Prof Khaleeq Anjum, Delhi in 1990, Volume I): 'Quwwatal-Islam Masjid'd Din Sam alias Shihabu'd-Din Ghori, conquered Delhi in AH 587 corresponding to

AD 1191 corresponding to 1248 Bikarmi, this idol-house (of Rai Pithora) was converted into a mosque. The idol was taken out of the temple. Some of the images sculptured on walls or doors or pillars were effaced completely, some were defaced. But the structure of the idol-house kept standing as before. Material from twenty-seven temples, which were worth five crore and forty lakh of Dilwals, were used in the mosque, and an inscription giving the date of conquest and his own name was installed on the eastern gate.'

'When Malwah and Ujjain were conquered by Sultan Shamsu'd-Din in AH 631 corresponding to AD 1233, then the idol-house of Mahakal was demolished and its idols as well as the statues of Raja Bikramajit were brought to Delhi, they were strewn in front of the door of the mosque.'

The relish with which the founder of Aligarh Muslim University wrote this, is indeed striking. At that time, Calcutta was still the capital of India. Had it been Delhi, his pleasure might perhaps have been greater. For the Raisina Hill from where India is governed, is only a few miles from Mehrauli where this monument to Hindu humiliation still stands.

Instant Vandalism

In 60 hours, a set of splendid temples at Ajmer were converted into a mosque. A furlong beyond the dargah of Khwaja Moinuddin Chisti is the triple temple complex built by an ancestor of Prithviraj Chauhan. The complex also contained the Sanskrit pathshala or school founded by the same Chauhan Vigraharaja III around 1158 AD. He was an avid literateur who wrote plays. One of these called *Harakeli Natak* was carved on plates of black stones which are even today displayed in the Rajputana Museum in the Akbar Fort in Ajmer. Also, on exhibition are rows of pretty carvings numbering about a hundred, brought from the complex. Another drama written by a court poet Somadev was similarly found. The sand stone statuettes have survived nearly 900 years except that the faces of all the figures were hacked out systematically. The temple complex also has a long store room which houses more of the many pretty relics. The lesser relics litter the compound as if they are there for anyone to take away.

This mosque, called 'Adhai Din Ka Jhopra', is a ready

object of shuddhi or purification to again becoming a temple. Certainly that is what Alexander Cunningham implied. In the Archaeological Survey of India (ASI) report written by him in 1864-65, Cunnigham found it difficult to follow some parts of the plan of the Quwwatul Islam mosque at Delhi, but says that nearly every part of the plan of the Ajmer mosque is still traceable, so that the original design of the architect can be restored without much difficulty. Externally it is a square of 259 feet on each side, with four peculiar star-shaped towers at the corners. There are only two entrances, one to the east and the other to the south, the north side being built against the scarped rock of the hill. The interior consists of a quadrangle 200 feet by 175 feet, surrounded on all four sides by cloisters of Hindu pillars. The mosque itself, which forms the western side of the quadrangle, is 259 feet long by 57½ feet broad, including the great screen wall, which is no less than 11-12 feet thick and 56 feet high.

The complex is, for the last 800 years, popularly known as 'Adhai Din Ka Jhopra' (the shed of two and a half days). This is so called, because the three temples here were converted into a masjid over only two and a half days. After the second battle of Tarain in 1192 AD, in which Shahabuddin Muhammad Ghori defeated and killed Prithviraj Chauhan, the victor passed through Ajmer. He was so awed by the temples that he wanted them destroyed and replaced instantly. He asked Qutbuddin Aibak, his slave general, to have the needful done in 60 hours' time so that he could offer prayers in the new masjid on his way back.

The *Jhopra* is among the first in a series of temple desecrations perpetrated by foreign rulers of India. The earlier atrocities were by Mahmud of Ghazni, who raided but did not stay back to rule. The triple temples were so attractive that the desecrator chose to retain all, or most of the pillars. There are 70 of them under three roofs, which meet and appear to be one integrated whole. And there are other pillars beyond the covered edifice, which looks like a pavilion in splendid stone.

The pillars are some 30 feet high, gorgeously carved either with exquisite designs up to a height of about 26 feet, thereafter adorned with delicate figurines. Uncannily, there is not a single figure whose face has not been cut off. Nowhere in Europe does one see such acts of vandalism, except what the original barbarian *vandals* themselves perpetrated under their king Gaiseric, in the wake of the conquest of Rome in 455 AD. Hereafter, the word vandal became synonym with wilful desecration and destruction. The figurines on all the relics on display at the Rajputana Museum, as well as those salvaged by the Archaeological Survey of India (ASI) and duly locked in the compound of the *Jhopra,* have been systematically defaced. Amongst the thousands of stone heads, not a single nose or an eye is visible.

Mind you, the ASI has done nothing to excavate or salvage anything in the complex since independence. With the passing of the Protection of National Monuments Act, 1951 (see Annexure II), all archaeological activities have been frozen. The credit for the excavations goes to Cunningham and DR Bhandarkar; during the first half of the 20thcentury by the latter. Details are available in the Rajasthan District Gazetteer, Ajmer, 1966.

Muhammad Ghori presumably offered prayers within the stipulated two-and-a-half days. Subsequently, in about 1200 AD the Adhai Din Ka Jhopra was completed with a well-carved façade, which is best described in the words of the ASI Report for 1893: 'The whole of the exterior is covered up with a network of tracery so finely and delicately wrought that it can only be compared "to a fine lace."' Cunningham described the exterior of the Jhopra even more eloquently: 'For gorgeous prodigality of ornament, beautiful richness of tracery, delicate sharpness of finish, laborious accuracy of workmanship, endless variety of detail, all of which are due to the Hindu masons, this building may justly vie with the noblest buildings which the world has yet produced.'

To come back to Hindu sculptures, Mulkraj Anand has said: 'This relief in Ajmer Museum is carved of intricately related figures, obviously intended for decorative effect. It rises above mere adornment by the delicate application of the chisel to achieve a composition which is compact and balanced.' But there was no mention even by him of the pathos of defacement and desecration. In fact, there is nothing either compact or balanced about the edifice. The exterior added by Aibak and his successors comprises carvings of the verses from the Quran on a yellow and distinctly softer stone, compared to the Hindu edifice behind it. This crudity of effort is overlooked by Mulkraj Anand.

Such then was the vandalism with which the sultanate in Delhi began. The Quwwatul Islam masjid next to the Qutb Minar, which was also built by Sultan Aibak, and the Adhai Din Ka Jhopra at Ajmer, are examples of desecration committed with a plain intent. Both are indelible specimens of humiliation perpetrated by the victor upon the vanquished.

The Ataladevi and other Masjids of Jaunpur

In 1403 AD, Ibrahim Naib Barbak ordered all Hindus to quit the city of Jaunpur, so that only Muslims could live there. Hindu temples in the town were demolished, to be replaced by mosques.

During Sultan Ibrahim's regime, Hindus were prohibited from openly worshipping idols, sounding *nakkus*, and leaving their houses in the rainy season for the purpose of burning their dead on the banks of the river near the city. He also levied a tax on them, and at length, in the year of the Hijri 806 or AD 1403-04, ordered them to leave Jaunpur, and to live elsewhere in its vicinity. Their houses were given to adherents of the faith (Islam), and the Hindus, being without friend or aid, were forced to abandon their homes and reside in the circumjacent villages. This is quoted from Khair-ud-din's *History of Jaunpur* translated by Pogson and reported by Cunningham.

The reason for Cunningham's reference to the holy city of Mecca in comparison with Jaunpur was to stress his conviction that Mohammedans did their work of destruction with unusual thoroughness. Today, there is no trace whatsoever of any old Hindu temple standing in Jaunpur. As is well known, the holy city of Mecca has no place of worship other than mosques. Nor are any non-Muslims allowed to enter Mecca.

Khair-ud-din, in his *History of Jaunpur,* observed that the Sultan then ordered the destruction of the Dewal (temple) Atala, the Dewal of Bijay Mandal and the Dewal of Chachakpur. He also commanded mosques to be built on their foundations. He ordered Bijay Mandal to be converted into the Khalis-Mukhlis and Chachakpur into the*Jhanjhari* (chain like) masjid.

The *Gazetteer* of Jaunpur district (1908), written by HR Neville, the district collector of Jaunpur, confirms that the temple was demolished by Ibrahim Naib Barbak, the brother of Sultan Firoz Shah Tughlaq who erected the Jhanjhari masjid in honour of a saint called Hazrat Ajmali. Not far from Jhanjhari is what is popularly known as the Ataladevi masjid. On two sides, in front of this rectangular edifice, are rows of two-storey cloisters. Opposite the mosque is also a similar cloister, which now houses a madarsa. According to the *Gazetteer*, there stood an equally large temple built by Raja Vijaya Chandra of Kannauj, the father of Jaichand. The temple was demolished by Khwaja Kamal Khan in 1364 AD and the mosque completed by Ibrahim in 1408 AD. Several dates were inscribed on the pillars which, incidentally, are the same as those that belonged to the temple. The cloisters on all the three sides, with a 174 square feet courtyard in the middle, belonged to the temple. Neville has quoted Cunningham in this regard.

Yet another temple turned mosque is the *Char Ungli*, four fingers or Khalis-Mukhlis masjid. On the left of its main gate is a space for a small stone in which the four fingers of any hand fit exactly, whether of a child or a grown-up. It was believed to have miraculous powers whereby wishes are fulfilled and curses come true. The original stone is missing; the space has been filled by a substitute.

Mukhlis and Khalis were in turn governors of Jaunpur under Ibrahim Naib Barbak, who was anxious to build an edifice for the residence of a celebrated saint named Saiyid Usman of Shiraz, who had fled from Delhi during Timur's invasion. In 1908, when the *Gazetteer* was published by Neville, the descendants of the saint still resided near the mosque. The style of architecture is not very different from that of the Jhanjhari masjid. The roof stands on ten rows of Hindu temple pillars. According to the *Gazetteer*, the mandir had been built by Raja Vijaya Chandra.

The river Gomti flows through the town of Jaunpur with an impressive bridge across it. It is a massive stone structure built in the 1560s. The bridge does not rise towards its centre but is flat. An original construction, the only feature marring its originality is a colossal stone lion standing over a small elephant. According to Neville, it bears the stamp of ancient Hindu workmanship and must have adorned the gateway of some building erected by the Raja of Kannauj.

To the west of the northern end of the bridge is the big fort of Jaunpur, built in the time of Ibrahim. But Firoz Shah Tughlaq is credited with having rebuilt the fortress on an old structure inherited from the Hindu era. Evidence of the legacy is the masjid inside the fort, built on temple pillars of various shapes and designs. Neville has remarked that some of the pillars are upside down which supports the theory that a number of temples in Jaunpur were destroyed in order to provide stones required to build the fort; the inner face of almost every stone bore carvings, which had decorated Hindu temples.

My visit to Jaunpur turned out to be a tragi-comedy of errors. I went to see the temple built by Jaichand's father but instead could see only the iconoclastic exploits of Ibrahim

Naib Barbak and Firoz Shah Tughlaq. I wondered what could have motivated medieval rulers to carry out such acts of vandalism. My dismay deepened when I read the *Gazetteer* written by Neville, an English Christian. He lamented that the work of demolition was so complete that hardly a vestige remains of this early epoch; but it is clear that Jaunpur must have been a place of considerable size at any rate, in the days of the last Hindu kings of Kannauj.

Vrindavan Restored by the British

A temple was beheaded only for the ego of Aurangzeb.

The temple today is 55 feet tall. Before its upper part was destroyed on Aurangzeb's orders in anticipation of his visit to Vrindavan in 1670 AD, the mandir was reputed to be twice that height. On its roof, after the destruction, a *mehrab* or prayer wall was erected and the emperor offered *namaaz.* Almost two centuries later, FS Growse, who belonged to the Bengal Civil Service and was Collector of Mathura District, had the mehrab removed. First, because it was an eyesore, and second, in an endeavour to redeem whatever character was left of the temple. Although the original idol remained at Jaipur, another set of deities was installed by the pujaris or priests. Since then, the temple has a flat roof. Probably, no other desecrated temple had been the subject of so much repair and refurbishment by British rulers. Of supreme importance was the fact of the mandir being restituted to Hindu devotees. It was the greatest act of shuddhi or purification, although performed before Swami Dayanand Saraswati reintroduced Vedic procedures.

Growse, therefore, deserves a place in the hall of Hindutva.

The Gobind Dev temple at Vrindavan, Mathura, is indeed massive; its plinth is 105 feet by 117 feet. It is estimated that the original height was about 110 feet without which it would not have been possible to see the mashaal or torch either from Agra or from Delhi. The temple was built in 1590 AD by Maharaja Mansingh of Jaipur.

The Gobind Dev temple is also unique for two other reasons but we shall come to these a little later. For the satisfaction of its desecrators, the celia, or the sanctum sanctorum, was destroyed. Fortunately, the idol of Shri Krishna or Gobind had been removed to Jaipur by the pujaris in anticipation of Aurangzeb's impending visit in 1670 AD; the emperor was already notorious as an iconoclast. The roof of the truncated edifice was to be reserved for namaaz. No sooner had the mehrab been constructed, as illustrated in the photograph in *History of Indian and Eastern Architecture* by James Fergusson, Aurangzeb inaugurated it himself by offering prayers.

All except two statuettes were defaced, including the one at the door of what is now the temple, after crossing the foyer hall. The destruction was not confined to the upper floors. It extended to the hundreds of statuettes that even today adorn the temple walls outside as well as inside, the ceilings or doors. The vandals overlooked two small statuettes, one of Shri Krishna and the other of Radha, on the outside of the left wall as one faces the temple.

An American historian of Indian architecture, George Mitchell, has concluded that the original sanctum sanctorum was destroyed. In his words: 'Once the *garbhagriha* had been torn down, there was little point in further wreckage... It seems to me that only those with some understanding of the ritual significance of the garbhagriha would have been capable of desecrating a temple in this careful manner.'

Prof R Nath introduces the subject of the Gobind Dev

temple by quoting Aurangzeb's decree of April, 1669: 'Eager to establish Islam, (Aurangzeb) issued orders to the governors of all the provinces to demolish the schools and temples of the infidels and with the utmost urgency put down the teaching and the public practice of the religion of these unbelievers. The great temple of Gobind Dev fell a victim to iconoclastic vandalism within a year of the decree. Its inner sanctum and its superstructure were almost entirely destroyed. The main hall was also damaged. Sculpted figures on the *dvarasakha* were literally defaced.'

The temple has yet another unique feature. Quoting an article in the *Calcutta Review,* Growse says: 'Aurangzeb had often remarked about a very bright light shining in the far distant, in the south east horizon and in reply to his enquiries regarding it, was told that it was a light burning in a temple of great wealth and magnificence at Vrindavan. He accordingly resolved that it should be put out and soon after, sent some troops to the place who plundered and threw down as much of the temple as they could and then erected on the top of the ruins a mosque wall where, in order to complete the desecration, the emperor is said to have offered up his prayers.'

Incidentally, the canopy standing on four pillars, which must have acted as a shed for the burning torch or mashaal, is lying on the ground at the back of the present sanctum sanctorum. It was so fixed, presumably by Growse in the 1870s. It has no relevance to the temple's architecture. This reinforces the belief that this canopy belonged to the top of the once towering temple.

While Aurangzeb's ego might have been gratified, the desecration took with it what is described by Fergusson as one of the most elegant temples in India, and the only one perhaps, from which a European architect might borrow a few hints. What did Growse have to say about this? 'I should myself have thought that solemn or imposing was a more appropriate term than elegance for so massive a building and that the suggestions that might be derived from its study were many rather than few.'

A number of motives have been attributed to the invaders who desecrated temples, such as looting of treasures, subduing the populace by arousing dread, informing the area that a sultan had replaced the raja. There is, however, no other instance of a temple being desecrated because it defied the ego of an emperor.

Henry Hardy Cole has written: 'I am not sure that the restoration of the upper-most parapet is correct and think that it would have been better to leave the superstructure, as it appeared when I first saw it, with all the evidence of Aurangzeb's destructive hand.'

Incomplete Shuddhi

Ayodhya is also an example of shuddhi, albeit incomplete, until a permanent Ram Lalla mandir is built. We do not know when we will overcome the controversies and when we shall be able to start building the temple. It is a simple issue. Most Hindus believe that Shri Rama was born in Ayodhya; it is a matter of faith. Most Muslims accept that Mir Baqi built the Babri edifice as a tribute to the new conqueror, Babar. In 1528 AD, there was hardly any Muslim resident in the city of Shri Rama. There were plenty of temples, but no mosque. Even today there are not many Muslims who live in the vicinity, until one gets to Faizabad, several kilometres away.

For decades, the edifice was not used by Muslims. In any case, the so-called Babri Masjid was one among thousands upon thousands of mosques in India. It had no special sanctity, whereas for the Hindus the birthplace of Shri Rama is of infinite sentimental value. The obvious gesture should have been to gracefully hand over the edifice to Hindu devotees. But no! Some leaders formed a Babri Masjid Action Committee, when no political party had espoused the Hindu cause, thus politicising the issue. Unfortunately, the Hindu leadership did not voice home truths. Instead, they got bogged down in responding to the Muslim claim point for point, argument by argument.

The first home truth was the contrast between what Ayodhya means to the Hindu sentiment and how comparatively insignificant it is to Muslims. The second truth to pose is: how would Muslims react to a Hindu proposal to build a temple in either Mecca or Medina? The third home truth is that the Christians commemorate the birth of Jesus Christ at Bethlehem by having erected the Church of Nativity. Muslims have left it alone presumably as a mark of respect for Christian sentiments. Khalifa Hakeem Bi Amr Illah destroyed the church of the Holy Sepulchre in Jerusalem during 1009 AD but did not touch the Church of Nativity at Bethlehem. Surely, the Muslims in the 21st century should be more considerate than the khalifa a thousand years ago. But they are not.

Instead of dealing with petty, self-seeking leaders, Hindu spokesmen should have addressed the Muslim masses, frankly and openly. But the initiative was allowed to remain with the Government of India; rather, the then prime minister who had a vested interest in allowing the controversy to persist between the spokesmen and petty leaders, without allowing either side to win. If the petty ones had succeeded in preserving the edifice, the political dividend might have eventually accrued to the likes of Viswanath Pratap Singh or Mulayam Singh Yadav. At the same time, for Prime Minister Narasimha Rao, it was best that the mosque edifice was out of the way. A Hindu metaphor says if there is no bamboo, there can be no flute to play!

The Demolition

Hype was therefore allowed to be generated. It became evident to the public that the spokesmen were desirous of pulling down the edifice in order to build a new temple. I was in Ayodhya between 10.45 am and 5.45 pm on that fateful day. The whole township around the Babri edifice was choc-a-bloc with around two to three lakh people, most of whom had come from outside for *kar seva*. The whole day was spent on the terrace of a newish small building at a distance of what looked like a furlong from the edifice. Two of the domes were clearly visible, while the third one was covered by tall trees from where I was located.

Short speeches, interspersed by the singing of devotional songs, were all that was happening until about noon. A microphone was on the terrace and a few persons took turns to address the mass of karsevaks. No doubt the atmosphere was charged with expectations, but there was no apparent action. Then I saw youngsters climbing the domes and scratching them. In the course of the next hour, the surface of the domes had become the colour of sand; it had been a dirty black earlier. While the youngsters on top were exhilarated, crowds below uttered cries of thrill from time to time. For anyone who had the leisure to think, it was obvious that this was hardly the way to demolish the structure.

Around this time, two photographers ran to the terrace and complained that some five of them had been manhandled and the camera of one of them had been snatched and smashed. I concluded that the target was not the photographers but the cameras, since the kar sevaks inside the edifice were anxious not to be photographed. They were using crowbars to attack the top of the walls on which the domes rested. The objective must have been to weaken the base of the domes sufficiently for them to collapse. This too I heard from the photographers, as the terrace was too far away. Around 2.30 pm a dull thud was heard, followed by the crowd shouting in delight. This was presumably when the dome collapsed, but that was not visible from the terrace.

The chanting of *bhajans* and the shouting of slogans continued with the help of the mike on the terrace which was packed not only with sympathisers but also many police officers. There were many policemen in uniform in Ayodhya. They, however, had little to do since the kar sevaks on duty were making sure that there was no disorder. In fact, the only incident of manhandling of a person during the whole day was that concerning the photographers. One could now see a stream of young kar sevaks bringing away small pieces of debris to take home as souvenirs.

Then suddenly at 3.40 pm one of the two remaining domes collapsed. This time there was clapping. The cries of delight could be heard with the mass clapping. The scene on the terrace had to be seen to be believed. Jubilation was uncontrolled and many tears of joy were shed at Ayodhya on that day. At 4.30 pm, the third dome fell and for a while the birth town of Shri Rama saw a riot of exhilaration. Over the centuries, thousands of temples had been desecrated across north India. At last, the Hindus present felt that they had got back at least one of them.

As the sun was receding on the short winter day, it was getting cold and the kar sevaks began to melt away from the Ramjanmabhoomi. I left the terrace at 5.30 pm and was back in my car before 5.45 pm. Soon after, I heard on the radio that the Chief Minister had resigned and subsequently his ministry had been dismissed and Governor's Rule imposed in Uttar Pradesh by the central government.

On the way back to Lucknow, many scenes kept coming back to my mind. The one scene that kept recurring the most, was that of the huge edifice, tall and with thick walls standing without domes. At the little motel in Lucknow, probably at 9.30 pm or 10.00 pm, I heard Prime Minister Narasimha Rao speaking on TV. The PM condemned the demolition as a dirty and shameful act and promised to rebuild the Babri masjid. I, therefore, wondered before falling asleep, whether the central government would replace the three domes post haste. The whole of the next day was spent in driving back to Delhi.

On the 10th morning, most of the newspapers had a photograph of a small flat little temple with a tiny flag flying at its centre. This was the temple built quickly by the central government on the site of the demolished edifice for the Ram Lalla idol which, incidentally, I had the privilege to see on the terrace of the building I was positioned on, on the afternoon of 6 December. A pujari or priest had brought the black idol to the terrace in his anxiety to save it from the crashing domes.

Seeing the photograph of the new Ram Lalla temple, I realised that the central government had demolished the walls of the edifice. I was thunderstruck by the hypocrisy of the secular government of India which had promised to rebuild the masjid. The government, instead, had demolished the walls in a matter of 60 hours between the evening of the 6th and the morning of the 9th when this photograph must have been taken. *No picture of the Babri edifice sans its domes has been seen by anyone I know. Evidently, Ayodhya was cordoned off while the walls were demolished and the debris removed with extraordinary dispatch.*

I said to myself: even if I could not help a friend to rebuild his broken roof, at least, I would not go to the friend's house and demolish the walls. But that is what the central government did at Ayodhya in December 1992.

The Origin of Hindutva

The seed of Hindutva can be said to have been sown about 3,400 years ago by Shri Krishna, who dreamt of a pan India and who sent his message as far as the present day Waziristan in the north, Manipur in the east and Tamil Nadu in the south.

It is true that the expression 'cultural nationalism' is regarded to have been first used by Raj Narain Bose, the grandfather of Maharshi Aurobindo, way back in the 19th century. This, however, should not lead anyone to believe that Hindutva is as recent as that. Nor was it a reaction against either Islamic or Christian pressure. The basic inspiration was that the whole of India, despite all its diversity, was essentially one. The significance of the word cultural is also to distinguish this nationalism from a 'religious' impulse. Even today, the central thrust of Hindutva is national unity.

The concept of nationalism, as distinct from mere unity, is comparatively new. Its seed was sown by the Reformation which overtook Christianity in 16th century Europe. The plant, however, blossomed some two centuries later with the rise of the mercantile class, as distinct from the landed aristocracy, quite a part of which was the clergy that controlled the churches of Europe. The inspirational base of nationalism became useful in reducing the power of the monarchy. In fact, until the advent of nationalism, there was little by way of a political ideology except as provided by religion or rather Christianity.

Nevertheless, the desire of the Indian civilisation to underline its unity was first demonstrated as long ago as some 3,400 years. It was Krishna who first personified the unity of India. On his shifting from Mathura to Dwarka, Krishna went on to become president of the Andhaka-Vrishni league or confederation of Yadava republican committees. They were situated on the west coast of what is now called Saurashtra, the great peninsula in Gujarat.

The area was called Prabhas and the capital was at Dwarkapuri. The city of Prabhas Patan still throbs with life and activity. It is only a few kilometres from Somnath. The constituent members of the Andhaka-Vrishni league had their differences and could not pull together. Krishna was keen to ensure unity but his efforts eventually came to naught. (*The Republican Trends in Ancient India* by Shobha Mukherji; published by Munshiram Manoharlal, 1969)

Realising he was ahead of his time and, yet being wedded to the idea of political unity, Krishna charted a new path. He guided and supported the Pandavas in the epic Kurukshetra War. Eventually they emerged victorious and established a united kingdom at Hastinapura. Soon thereafter, Yudhishthira was advised to perform the *Aswamedha* or the horse sacrifice with the typical intent of expanding the state (*The History and Culture of the Indian People* edited by RC Majumdar; published by Bhartiya Vidya Bhavan).There is now a general consensus of opinion in favour of the historicity of Krishna.

Having failed to achieve political oneness with the help of republics forming a confederation, Krishna evidently went on to support King Yudhishthira to consolidate a united kingdom, presumably in hope of promoting an expanding unification. The presumption is based on the universal adoration Krishna personally received then and which is perpetuated to this day.

Everyone, at least in India, realises what Krishna means to the Hindu psyche.

No doubt, Krishna is more woven into the soul of Indians than any other avatar. The *Bhagvad Gita* is a gem of a philosophy, not a religious commandment, nor even a piece of mythology. Krishna was predominantly a strategist whether in diplomacy or war. His soul was evidently wedded to a united India. Else, how could he still be adored literally from Kashmir to Kanyakumari and from Kamrup to Kutch? Manipuris on the Myanmar border are predominantly devotees of Krishna. It is believed that Arjuna had visited this border State whose princess Chitrangada was married to him. Arjuna was also reputed to have conquered a number of other territories. Similarly, his younger brother Nakula went westwards and made quite a few conquests on the banks of river Sindhu as well as Saraswati. Incidentally, the south was also not neglected; all the Iyengars of Tamil Nadu are devotees of Krishna, being Vaishnavites. In Tamil, Krishna is called Kanna and Kannan is quite a popular name.

What else is this but cultural nationalism or Hindutva? Having accepted Krishna as the fountainhead or rather the Gangotri of Hindutva, let us move to Vishnugupta Kautilya in the 4th century BC. A great deal of his life and work are mixed between the light of history and the mist of legend. Traditionally, the Hindu is more a speaker or listener; less a reader and writer. In the event, ancient history has been less recorded than could be. Else, we might have discovered more figures who personified Hindutva. However, let us get back to the recorded history.

Kautilya was the friend, guide and philosopher to

Chandragupta Maurya who was the greatest emperor that the subcontinent had known until then. He ascended the throne of Magadha at Pataliputra in 321 BC. In the context of Hindutva, Chandragupta's achievements were several. He defeated and expelled all foreigners, specifically the Greek conquerors and their garrisons from the soil of India. His empire comprised all of north and a large part of eastern India. There was an urge for a pan-Indian oneness. The brain behind this was Kautilya's, while the brawn was the emperor's, whose grandson Ashoka carried the march forward.

Ashoka's empire was larger than his grandfather's but for the purpose of Hindutva, we are not concerned with kingly or imperial success. The question is who inspired or initiated a new drive towards the oneness of India. Credit for this must go to Adi Sankaracharya, who did a great deal more than all the emperors put together.

Although there is a controversy about the century in which the Acharya lived his 32 hectic years, circumstantially we take it to be 8thcentury AD (*Adi Sankara—His Life and Times* by TMP Mahadevan and published by the Bharatiya Vidya Bhavan). He is believed to have been an avatar of Lord Shiva. For the purpose of Hindutva, however, our interest is confined to his consciousness as to the oneness of India.[5] And the fact that he travelled the length and breadth of the subcontinent more than once was no easy task to have been undertaken on foot for someone who was based in Kalady in Kerala. He established the four *dhams*, namely, Dwarka, Badrinarh, Puri and Kanchi. The mission of Adi Sankara went a long way in proving the essential integrity of India. He is an important link in the long chain of Hindutva.

5 Adi Sankara undertook his mission to rejuvenate Hinduism, very aware that Islam was striking at India's doors from many directions. Its first mosque had been built very close to his birthplace. The Cheraman Juma Mosque is a mosque in Methala, Kodungallur Taluk, Thrissur District. Built in 629 AD, it is the first mosque in India. It was built by Malik Deenar, an Arab propagator of Islam.

The Hindu Vision of Polity and Governance

Many a dreamer has chased the ideal state, but thus far it has proved a mirage. Su-raaj or a good state is an aspiration as old as civilisation. More often than not, in India we have called it Rama Rajya. Gandhi certainly did, but he did not define it just as no one before him did. Being a prescription for practical politics, this volume defines the goal for which the entire Hindu movement is striving. What follows immediately offers the definition of social, economic as well as political faces of su-raaj. At the core of su-raaj lies the *rule of dharma*, which requires leaders to be more ethical than others. In contrast, under the rule of law, all have equal obligations.

A Muslim cleric's mind would naturally flash to the idea of *Dar-ul-Islam,* or what is also often described as *Nizam-e-Mustafa* (the system of the Prophet), an ideal which was born with Islam and has lived with most devout Muslims. Similarly, many a socialist intellectual may look upon the call of Rama Rajya as a bugle of revivalism. This would be a case of looking at a Hindu ideal with a Marxist mind.

Rama personifies dharma. Whereas *rajya* means the state whose essential function is to enable each citizen to perform his dharma without let or hindrance by other people. Every citizen is assured of justice in Rama's rule. Dharma is the trinity of faith, duty and morality.

There is nothing particularly Hindu about dharma.

After all, which civilised human being can deny that he has a faith to cherish and a duty to perform? Or, one can put it this way: an *imaan* to cherish and a *farz* towards others. Each citizen has the right to follow his dharma. At the same time, he/she has the obligation to allow every other citizen to abide by his/her dharma. The fundamental function of Rama Rajya is to ensure that every citizen has the freedom to fulfil himself/herself and at the same time, not to obstruct any other citizen from fulfilling himself/herself. That is justice.

For one citizen to be just to another, he/she should be prepared for some self-denial, if not also sacrifice, from time to time. Rama was the epitome of sacrifice. As a gesture of his duty towards his father, he gave up fourteen years of his life in exile or *vanvaas*. For the sake of his principles, he gave up his wife, Sita. The king or the queen could not afford to carry any blemish. It is worth recalling that a washerman had cast doubt on Sita's chastity during her custody at Lanka.

The moral of Rama's sacrifice was that the higher placed an individual, the greater the demand on his conduct. He should not only behave ideally but also be seen to be ideal so as to ensure credibility without which a king or leader cannot command implicit respect. And without which no state can aspire to be perfect. There is nothing religious, communal or Hindu about this.

The essence of Rama Rajya is the rule of dharma. The higher a citizen is placed, the greater is the demand on his/her probity. For example, for anyone it should be sufficient to be honest. But for a minister it might be essential to be seen and known to be honest. If any reasonable doubt is cast even on the integrity of his associates, however near or dear, he must distance himself from the persons, as indeed Rama did from his beloved Sita. Yet, as a tribute to his faith in her fidelity, he did not marry again, nor allow any other woman to occupy a place in his life.

The conscientious soul that he was, Rama must have experienced exceptional agony. But the duty of kingship superseded the love of a husband for his wife. Rama has been criticised as being unfair not only to Sita but also to his mother Kausalya, who was so devastated at Rama's exile that she wanted to accompany him in vanvaas. But, he turned down her wish to share his travails and left her behind at Ayodhya. If he were only a husband or a son, the criticism would be justified.

But the call of the king and country is greater than the duty to mother and wife. This, in fact, is the core of the difference between the rule of dharma and the rule of law, which the Anglo-Saxon world of the British and the Americans is so proud of. The rule of law insists on everyone, high or humble, being equal before the law; whereas dharma differs from person to person, for king and commoner.

Justice should be progressive and not equal because individuals do not have equal responsibilities. The *karma*[6] of each soul is different; so is his or her *bhagya*.[7] If the deeds are different, so must be destinies. Each individual has the liberty to excel in his karma, there being no limits or ceilings on good deeds. At the same time, no one's endeavour to excel should be allowed to curb the efforts of others. Nor should an evildoer be permitted to disturb the karma of the other citizens. The more powerfully placed a person, the greater his ability to disturb others. Progressive justice must therefore be demanding on the

---

6 deeds.
7 fate.

powerful, the well-placed wrong doer and, at the same time, protective of the commoner.

Another outstanding feature of suraaj has to be a clean public life, as clean as is humanly possible. If the rule of dharma expects those in positions of power to be not only upright but also to be seen to be upright, the least that mere ordinary citizens can do is not to be corrupt. A major cause of corruption is the assumption of excessive functions by the state. More the functions a state assumes, more is the number of officers, not all of whom are above temptation. Suraaj, therefore, has to find an answer in providing a minimal government to the people.

In any case, the Hindu ethos is based on the liberty of the individual to perform his karma to the best of his ability. A welfare state or a socialist state are Western concepts emanating from the Christian belief that God made all men equal but society renders them unequal. The endeavour of a Christian's conscience, therefore, is serving and reforming society and to make men equal. If one cannot make a person rich, one should at least try and teach his children free or cure his sickness. Charity is an endeavour in that direction.

Liberty has to be curbed for the sake of trying to achieve equality. To that extent, liberty and equality stand at opposite ends of the scale. *For Indians, suraaj would have to be a state inspired by liberty, which means not only a democracy with complete freedom of expression but also a government which does not breathe down the necks of its citizens.*

Liberty should not be confused with licence for citizens to do what they like. *There is a clear dividing line between liberty and licence. The former is the freedom for every citizen to perform his karma. The latter is to tolerate a wayward citizen stepping on the toes of fellow citizens and obstructing them.* There should be no licence.

Minimal government provided by suraaj has to be slim and strict, so that no one is permitted to disturb the liberty of others to do their karmic best. A number of states were categorized by Gunnar Myrdal, the famous Swedish writer of *Asian Drama*, as soft. What he meant was that such a state had a weak government which was either run by corrupt leaders or which, at least, could not control corruption. Nor could it ensure the enforcement of law or order. Suraaj must be the opposite of a soft state.

Hindutva is Dialectical

Hindutva or Hinduness is dialectical, because logically, even state policies can be drawn from its core, much like yarn and cloth from a sliver of cotton. If the essence of the Hindu explanation of life is accepted as a premise, almost all life, socio-economic as well as political, flow logically. The basic tenets of the Hindu explanation are four:

- All living beings, humans, animals, birds, reptiles and worms, are parts of the Hindu universe.
- That each has a soul or a *jeevatma* whose endeavour is to strive and prove itself, albeit through a series of lives, elevated enough to mingle with the *paramatma* or the total soul.
- That the paths for achieving this salvation from the cycle of birth and rebirth are many. Each individual is free to choose his or her path.
- That while all jeevatmas endeavour to elevate themselves, upon death their souls transmigrate amongst the various living beings.

The Hindu ethos considers the individual as supremely important. Society and the state exist for the individual. Two of the three well known Hindu paths for the pursuit of *mukti* or salvation, namely the bhakti and the *gnana yoga*s, bypass society. For, one can be pursued through devotion or worship, with or without a temple; whereas the other can be practised by thought and meditation within or without an ashram. *Karmayoga* is the only path which must transit through society. Hinduism does not need a comprehensive code or message or, for that matter, an authoritative scripture, neither book nor manifesto.

Self actualisation (self-improvement or fulfilment), rather than social performance, is the central theme of Hinduism. The individual is free not only to pursue his own goal but also to cultivate any of his own aptitudes in order to fulfil himself. He may compete with his fellow beings or he may not. Neither comparison nor competition is induced by his faith. In other words, he does not have to run the rat race of success. He can easily make happiness his goal through self-fulfillment, as distinct from success.

Conceptually then, the average Hindu has little or non-existent interest or inclination in superintending or controlling his community or, for that matter, anyone else's. In fact, he does not seek the power to do so. This explains why Hinduism has never had, unlike Christianity, a network or hierarchy of priests. Priests, or pujaris or pandas are usually confined to the individual temple. Nor is there any mode or method of inducing others to become Hindus. The question of Hinduism controlling the state or government can never, therefore, arise. The question of conquering and colonising the territory of others is irrelevant. Imperial ambitions do not come naturally to the Hindu.

The Hindu inclination is to leave people alone. This preference for non-interference discourages any tendency in the Hindu towards autocracy or dictatorship. *To that extent, the average Hindu is amenable to democracy.* He is ready to concede the freedom of others to have a say in their affairs. It follows that he disapproves of intervention in his style of life. *Nor does centralisation fit in with the Hindu psyche.*

The Hindu's preference for non-violence, however, is rooted in the belief that every living being carries a part, however minute, of the paramatma. The theory of *samsara* or transmigration, only reinforces the Hindu reluctance to hurt or to kill. Carried to its logical conclusion, the jeevatma of one's departed parents or grandparents could be residing in the body of any animal, bird or another human being. This makes violence generally repugnant. The preference for a vegetarian diet is a corollary of this repugnance.

True, the opposite of violence is more than just nonviolence. It is tolerance or a ready acceptance of the rights of others to do their things in their own way. *Violence results from intolerance of the ways of others. This explains why, in many ways, Hinduness and tolerance are ideally synonymous.*

Can state policies flow from Hinduness? The answer is yes, because the ethos is dialectical. It has the potential for becoming a mainspring from which can flow policies appropriate with changing times. On analysis, it has been found that the description of Hinduness states that *imperial desire does not come naturally to the Hindu.* A country that does not have any desire to dominate another can only have a foreign policy that is confined to the maintenance of cordial relations with other countries so that no country is easily provoked to attack. Its citizens across the world can then enjoy respect and protection, and its international commerce flows safely. Such a foreign policy needs a military designed essentially for defence, as distinct from offensive wars. The borders, the coastline and the skies over the country only have to be secured against aggression.

At home, the policy would lend itself to decentralised governance. Just as the individual is free to self actualise himself/herself, every little region of the country too should be allowed to fulfil itself. Thus the message of Hindutva is in favour of a federal structure as well as small states and small districts.

As all living beings are considered members of the Hindu universe, it follows that the environment should be so protected as to enable all of them to flourish. The *peepal* tree as an object of worship is symbolic of this concern for the ecology and in its turn is the basis of a policy for environment.

The concern for ecology logically extends to the need for a balance in population. Too many human beings can upset the balance. The animal population has declined and the current concern for wild life is a result of this unfortunate imbalance. *The ecological damage is not confined to the physical or the spiritual but also leads to poverty and misery.*

An aware Hindu should stand for a correction of this imbalance by, if necessary, a control on human birth. Conceptually, there should be no objection even to abortion as a means of birth control. True, a foetus has a body and life but it has no soul until it is born. Without the ability to perform karma, there can be no soul to a life. Abortion is therefore not a sin, unlike in Catholicism.

The dialectics of the ethos can lead one to a preference for a free market, as distinct from controls associated with welfarism, socialism or communism. Control militates against faith in liberty. There is an implicit promise of liberty of each citizen to participate in the market freely. In other words, the duty of society, or its representative in the state, is to ensure that no citizen takes the law into his hands and disturbs the liberty of anyone else. To this extent, the state must take interest in running the economy.

Nationalism

Nationalism should create national synergy, whereby the effort of four Indians will result in the output of, say, six. Some Indians might understand the concept of nationalism, but it bears iteration here that of the communities and religious groups that have operated on a world scale, it is the Christians world over who have contributed most to the evolution of nationalism and practised it as a political philosophy.

The Jews present a contrast to this. Most Jews, no matter where they live, candidly show their first sympathy for the idea of Israel. Until 1924, there was the Caliph, who was, at least symbolically, the spiritual as well as the temporal head of all Sunni Muslims. The communist is, *per se*, an internationalist owing his first loyalty to the 'workers of the world' rather than to his country.

Suraaj or good governance must be India's ultimate goal. The question is how to get there. There is no short cut and the only way to achieve the objective is with the help of nationalism. Unless India becomes nationalist, it is going to be well nigh impossible to become modern, leave alone a suraaj. And what is nationalism? To put it simply, a nation is the extension of a joint family. It is the macro or the enlargement of what is micro or small, as represented by a family.

Most people usually have a common tradition and a shared memory, often called a common consciousness. Usually they speak the same language and worship similar gods, but this is not necessarily so. When someone in a family marries a woman from another part of the country or the world, she may speak a different language and profess a different faith. But she can still be very much an integral part of the family. The ultimate test of her membership is her loyalty to the family.

In exchange for this loyalty and love, the individual experiences a sense of belonging and a sense of security. The family roof offers shelter and protection. The family's goodwill gives the individual an identity, legitimacy and respectability. To belong to a nation, therefore, is to save oneself from the loneliness of an orphan or the diffidence which is often associated with an illegitimate child.

Property, whether land or building, gives the joint family a physical base. It provides a material bond to the members and the promise of a refuge in times of adversity. Similarly, the nation's property is territory. Without it, the nation disperses just as the joint family disintegrates when it does not have its land or buildings. The Jewish nation is a classic example. After its diaspora or dispersal from Palestine over 40 centuries ago, known in history as the Exodus,[8] the Jewish people had no territory. They dispersed to settle as far away as India, Iran, Russia, Germany, Poland and the USA.

The ill treatment of the Jews has a long history. Anti-Semitism is a common expression. Except in India, they were discriminated against everywhere. In Europe, they could neither own land nor get state employment. The climax of their tragedy was the extermination of six million Jews by Adolf Hitler during World War II (the Holocaust). What a colossal price for a people to pay for not possessing territory! This should be a useful reminder to those Indians who do not recognise the sanctity of our Motherland and who object to the prayer *Vande Mataram*.[9]

---

8 The Exodus , or departure of the Israelites from Egypt is framed in the timeline 1800 years BC. The Jews left Israel about 2000 years before Christ and moved again after Christ. So the migration of Jews span over about 5,000 years of recorded history. The first Jews in Kerala coast were sailors of King Solomon. There is reference to Black Jews of the South as early as 11th CE.

9 *Vande Mataram* is a poem written by Bankim Chandra Chattopadhyay in the 1870s, which he included in his 1881 novel *Anandamath*, whose context was the previous century's Sanyasi Rebellion. It was an Ode to Durga as the Mother Goddess, Shakti who gave strength to the warrior. Bengal interpreted mother here as Bangamata (Mother Bengal). The poem was composed into song by Rabindranath Tagore. Aurobindo first called it 'a National Anthem'. The first two verses of the song were adopted as the National Song of India in October 1937 by the Congress Working Committee.

After a long struggle, the Jews were able to acquire a part of Palestine as their territory. In 1948, the state of Israel was established with a small population including those who had been immigrating since 1882. It was indeed an old national dream at last come true. The Jews behaved like a nation possessed. With energy and determination, they built up a country of now six million Jews who inspire awe in the hearts of millions of Arabs across West Asia! Such is the magic of a motherland.

What is the practical value of nationalism? The answer is simple. No society has successfully graduated from the medieval, agrarian stage of history to the modern industrial era without the energy of nationalism. The communist countries were the exceptions which tried to take a historic leap into the modern age without the help of a nationalist spirit. In fact, they deprecated nationalism and claimed they were internationalist. Their call was for the workers of the world to unite.

The Soviet Union led this experiment which, as is well known, ended in disaster. The once-mighty Soviet Union, both the state and nation, collapsed like a pack of cards in December 1991. The failure was similar in its satellite countries of Europe. Be it Poland, Hungary, Czechoslovakia or Romania, all abandoned communism and its 'internationalist' plea. One must also observe the contrast between North and South Korea. Nationalism must not be confused with either liberalisation or democracy. The regime in Seoul, South Korea was autocratic until quite recently. The Chinese leadership after Mao Zedong was wise enough to see the point and to abandon its internationalist posture. Today, China is a picture of Han (their race) nationalism.

One may contrast the Russian disaster with the Japanese miracle. Japan is an island country with few natural resources and it is remarkable to see its aspiration to become the wealthiest nation on earth. This is the very country which suffered a severe defeat in World War II. The atomic bombing of Hiroshima and Nagasaki in 1945 is still green in global memory. As a people, the Japanese are extraordinarily single-minded in their purpose; to the extent of being obsessed by their objective. But that alone would not have taken them so far. What has made the overwhelming difference is their nationalism carried, as it were, to perfection in unity.

The whole nation has one supreme goal: to improve technology, make better and better products and to export more and more of them. What is unique is how the whole nation put its collective shoulder to the wheel of this supreme goal soon after the country's defeat in WWII.

Contrast India's stagnation with Japan's miracle. In 1945, India was better placed than the war-ravaged Land of the Rising Sun. Yet our country kept fumbling: going forward in some areas, backwards in others and marking time in many others. If there be one reason for this stagnation, it is the neglect of nationalism in the decades since Independence.

The collective memory or the consciousness of virtually all Indians is about the same. Whether described as Hindu or Indian, it amounts to the same. The ancestors of most Indians were Hindu at some point of time. Some communities like the Parsis came from Iran and have maintained their separate identity. But over the thousand years that they have been here, they have imbibed more than enough of the Indian ethos to be one with the rest and are equally Indian.

It is also true that a small percentage of the Muslims who came to India might not share the same consciousness. But even two or three centuries are not a short time. And who can claim to be of pure foreign blood? In any case, many of those who had strong non-Indian leanings migrated to Pakistan. There was no Islam even in most of what is now Pakistan until about the 13th century. Even Sind and Balochistan had none till after the coming of Mohammed bin Qasim in 712 AD.[10]

The essence of cultural nationalism was articulated by Sir Syed Ahmad Khan, the founder of the Aligarh Muslim University, in a speech he delivered in 1884.[11] 'Do you not inhabit the same land?' he asked. 'Remember that the words Hindu and Mohammedan are only meant for religious distinction—otherwise all persons, whether Hindu or Mohammedan, and even Christians who reside in this country, are all in this particular respect belonging to one and the same nation.' In another speech he referred to Hindus and Muslims as forming one nation. To a Punjabi Hindu audience, he said that every inhabitant of Hindustan is a Hindu, and added, 'I am therefore very sorry that you do not regard me as a Hindu.'[12] Later, ironically, Syed did a somersault and called Hindus and Muslims separate nations.

---

10 Alexander's army invaded India about 350 years BC. Records of the time say the Pauravas ruled the Punjab region at the time. This was an essentially Hindu kingdom. Megasthenes' records according to Greek historians Arrian, Diodorus, and Strabo, also describe the Hindu-Buddhist influence from the borders of Greece, Bactria to all of northern India. The Kushana empire was a syncretic empire, formed by the Yuezhi, in the Bactrian territories in the early 1st century. Later it spread up to near modern Varanasi. It was also a Hindu-Buddhist empire. Kanishka is dated to have ruled 127 CE to 140 CE.

11 *British Paramountcy and Indian Renaissance;* edited by RC Majumdar; page 309; Eminent Mussalmans page 32, Bharatiya Vidya Bhawan.

12 *India Divided;* Rajendra Prasad; page 99.

Hindutva's Strengths, Weaknesses, Opportunities and Threats

One should know oneself, one's strengths and weaknesses in the context of the task ahead. It is necessary to understand the environment in which one will have to operate and, above all, recognise the adverse factors that are possible to anticipate. In military parlance, this is called knowing the terrain and assessing probable enemies. It is only then that thinking should begin on the game plan for success.

The Strengths

The strengths of Hinduness bear iteration here. *Its greatest single strength is the wide horizon of its universe.* It spontaneously includes all humans regardless of their race or religion. Before the advent of the Muslims, everyone who came to India joined the Hindu fold. Immigrant, conqueror, or a camp follower, his group soon began to be treated as Hindus. The group retained its identity as a distinct caste like the Gujjar, Jat, Lohana, Meo et al. Each was free to choose his/her favourite avatar or deity like Krishna, Ram or Durga as well as his mode of worship.

A corollary of this universal view makes Hinduness inclusive of potentially anyone. There is no need for anyone to undergo conversion in order to espouse Hinduness. He/she can continue to worship in a church or a mosque and yet be in the mainstream. This is why Hindutva is translated as cultural nationalism with no religious connotation.

There are Christians who claim to be Brahmin and Muslims who also call themselves Rajput. Evidently, their collective memory overwhelms their current faith. All the children who love Mother India conceptually belong to the Hindu family. Only those who owe their allegiance beyond the borders of India are unwelcome. Their bodies might reside in the country but their souls yearn for say, Beijing or Islamabad.

The third strength of Hindutva is its infinite resilience. The ethos bends but does not break. Not flowing from the message of a prophet or the doctrine of a single holy book, Hindutva is neither rigid nor brittle. Hindu worship is so varied and decentralised to the last temple that it is well nigh unbreakable. This is unlike the Buddhist network of monasteries in ancient India, which were destroyed merely by killing the monks, as the invader often did. Another example of such vulnerability is the virtual wiping out of Christianity from Turkey. Although the headquarters of the Eastern Orthodox Church are still located at Istanbul, Christians today form less than two per cent of Turkey's population.

Yet another strength that flows from the lack of a prophetic message or a single scripture is the freedom from any finality. Hindutva can be open and ready to be amended in response to the challenge of changing time. The experience of a new *rishi* or the advent of a new discovery does not have to be ignored. The abolition of untouchability and the acceptance of contraception or birth control are examples. In the words of Sarvepalli Radhakrishnan, the unity of Hinduism is not one of an unchanging creed or a fixed deposit of doctrine, but is the unity of a continuously changing life. This makes Hinduness time dynamic.

Hindutva being dialectical, its potential offers scope for creativity. The evidence is the enormous contribution made by the Hindu civilisation during the pre-medieval centuries. Philosophy, mathematics, astronomy, sculpture, literature are some spheres in which remarkable creative work was done. Although Hindutva is based on spiritual inspiration, it can co-exist with science. A contradiction, like the one between the Bible and Charles Darwin with regard to the origin of species is not likely in the Hindu ethos. In fact, karma leading to bhagya or destiny is like a principle of physics: for every action, there is an equal and opposite reaction.

The original attitude towards womenfolk should prove to be another of Hindutva's strengths. For, it is the mother, and not the father, who really brings up the children. The quality of the future generations therefore, depends on the enlightenment of the women. During Vedic times, both boys and girls underwent the *Upanayana* or thread ceremony. Both studied the Vedas, which took 12 to 15 years. Marriage, therefore, had to wait until men and women were in their mid-twenties. The age difference between them was very little and they bore fewer children than they did later when the girls began to be married off early. The Mahabharata portrays the last phase of this Vedic tradition. Thereafter, a decline set in and women became unequal. Nevertheless, there was no *purdah*, women moved about more or less freely and were not an exploited species. Those evils crept in with the advent and fear of Islam.

Another particular strength of Hindutva is an entrepreneurial or business aptitude in a significant proportion of the people. Trading, banking and understanding the dynamics of money are traditional. This is an economic asset, both domestically and internationally.

An advantage in relationship with other countries is the Hindu preference for self-actualisation rather than a desire to control society, to dominate others and conquer colonies. If each country concentrated on self-actualisation, there can be no acquisitive or imperialistic tendency and therefore, little cause for tension or war.

The Weaknesses

It is important to dwell on the weaknesses of the Hindu ethos. In the process, a methodology that is popular in the field of management may be adopted. Managers call this a SWOT analysis. S stands for strengths, W for weaknesses, O for opportunities and T for threats. Political science does not often use this tool of analysis. It is interesting to see how far we get by trying this technique.

The purpose of identifying weaknesses is to make sure that they are removed or at least reduced as far as possible. For instance, Hindu tolerance is often misread for weakness, for its unwillingness to object or to resist. Similarly, non-violence is not understood by everyone. Some might even mistake it for cowardice. To them, non-violence impress only if the Hindu is first seen to use force.

The problem is not confined to the individual or the group but is magnified to the international level. Most countries, deliberately or implicitly, follow a policy of armed suasion, which means that the country should appear to be stronger than it is. But India has the image of being weaker than it is. The resulting confusion makes the conduct of relations with the others, whether countries or communities, unnecessarily difficult. When a Hindu argues over an issue with a Muslim, he could leave the latter confused. Indo-Pak dialogues also suffer from such impressions. This is all essentially at home since we in the subcontinent are mostly the same people. Imagine how foreigners of another continent are confounded.

Indian war record has been uneven. Led by the British or by officers trained in the British tradition, the Indian soldier has covered himself with glory. But prior to that, Indian armies have suffered more defeats than won victories. Leadership by Muslim kings made no difference. The defeat of Ibrahim Lodi by Babar in 1526 AD is an example. Nadir Shah and Ahmed Shah Abdali inflicted a similar fate on the Mughals, who were the progeny of Babar himself.

Ancient India has many an invention to its credit but hardly any in the sphere of war.[13] Evidently, Indian civilisation has taken insufficient interest in military affairs. There is comparatively little military literature or strategic discussion. This lacuna is not merely a Hindu characteristic. There are few political theories except what appears in the Mahabharata and Kautilya's *Arthashastra.* Hindutva has shown less interest in politics and governance than desirable, especially when one remembers that the subcontinent was invaded repeatedly. Little wonder that the British ruled nearly 40 crore Indians with not much more than a lakh of white men at a time.

The caste system is viciously divisive. It is a serious weakness which is difficult to overcome unless Hinduness rises to a strong enough identity to supersede the narrowness of casteism. There is nothing indelible about caste. It began as a surviving identity of a new settler group which was absorbed into the Hindu fold in ancient times. The Gujjars, Jats, etc. are examples. The broad classification of society into Brahmin, Kshatriya, Vaishya, Shudra and others was on professional lines like a division of labour. These were all perhaps relevant and useful in older times, but have now become obsolete and in fact, harmful.

One reason why caste has a special attraction to the Indian is perhaps his slavish complex developed over the last eight

13 Exception, perhaps was the Wootz steel, developed in the southern peninsular India, for swords in 600 BC.

centuries of alien rule. If a person does not belong to a top caste, it does not matter so long there is a caste below him. The Jatav is not desperate so long as there is the Valmiki below him. With perhaps a similar motivation, the Kapol bania caste in south Saurashtra has two sections, namely, 16 and 12. Although they intermarry, the 16 feel reassured that they are 'superior' to the 12!

Peering into one's weaknesses is seldom a pleasant experience. It hurts one's ego, which normally provides the driving force for effort to overcome and change. At the same time, the ego works as an opaque barrier between a person and his knowledge of himself and acts like a blind curtain of vanity between an illusion and what is real. In the process, many individuals go through life without knowing themselves. What is true of individuals is also true of groups of people or even a whole nation. It is therefore just as well that we tried to look at the weaknesses of Hinduness after enumerating its strengths.

One long historical phase has yielded place to another era. This change offers Hinduness a golden opportunity. The annals of fighting go back to the beginning of time. The concept of war, however, got crystallised with the advent of the feudal era, generally taken to be from the 9th to the 15th century AD.

The reason was that land was the fulcrum around which the polity as well as the economy revolved. On its surface grew crops and below the surface could be found valuable minerals. In between and around the land, there could be fishing. In other words, land came to be recognised as the principal source of wealth.

Every ambitious ruler extended his territory to as far as was possible without fighting. When it became necessary to fight, it was war. Territory added to the wealth and power of the state. When the ruler could not amalgamate the newly conquered territory into his own state, he made it into a colony; like British India, for example. Just as wars were fought in order to capture territory and acquire colonies, constant preparedness for war was required to defend and retain them. Individual rulers and dynasties yielded place to other forms of government but the primacy of territory and the importance of war continued for century after century.

A characteristic of Hinduness was its disinclination and distaste for fighting. Indian civilisation has many inventions to its credit ranging from medicine and surgery to mathematics and astronomy. But rarely does one hear of an Indian having invented a novel weapon or having innovated a new mode of fighting. The last victory against a true foreigner that one can remember in our annals was that of Chandragupta Maurya against Nicator Seleucus, the Macedonian general, left behind by Alexander in the 4th century BC. Incidentally, the modern-day fighting with Pakistan, which was a part of India until 1947, must be considered as merely a civil war.

Opportunity

As a follow-through of the Industrial Revolution, technology grew and with it the importance of manufacturing as a source of wealth. In due course, manufacturing overtook land in its ability to produce surpluses. The emphasis was on marketing which, in turn, made manufacturing more profitable. With revolutionary improvements in transport and communication, the world became increasingly smaller. International trade became simpler and exports became dominant in the economics of many countries. In the post World War II years, Japan and Germany proved exceptional in combining industrial technology with global marketing. To the extent that they overtook all other countries, except the USA.

Fifty years ago, Japan, after WWII's devastation, was distinctly a poorer economy than India. Its miracle also symbolises a new phase in history. Trade has replaced war as an instrument of attracting the surpluses of other economies.

Previously, an imperial country needed colonies to bring home surpluses of other economies. Japan did it by capturing markets rather than acquiring territory. The German miracle was also substantially engineered by exports. As it happened, both Germany and Japan lost territory after World War II. Germany was divided into two while Japan was deprived of Korea, Manchuria and several islands. Yet, they brought home more and more of, what we call in India, foreign exchange.

On the other hand, the great territorial giants, namely, the USA and the Soviet Union progressively built up foreign debts. The economy of the latter, as is well known, collapsed some years ago. Neither their natural resources nor their armies and arsenals made any economic impact. It can certainly be said that over the last five decades, goods have replaced guns and services have substituted soldiers as instruments of imperialism. There have been several regional wars since 1945 when the World War ended, but none of these has resulted in territories changing hands for economic considerations. Yes, China has occupied large tracts of our Aksai Chin. Israel has held the west bank of the river Jordan and until recently, held the Golan Heights of Syria. But all these occupations are for strategic reasons and not for economic gain. Trade then has largely replaced war.

Indians have traded for centuries.[14] Even when the British ruled and exploited our country, we enjoyed a trade surplus. In other words, the value of our exports exceeded the worth of our imports. The Indian businessman can read finance and the movement of money like the back of his palm. He is also a clever entrepreneur. When trading, he is in his element and that is just what the world wants today. With the advances in technology, and land ceasing to be the principal source of wealth, trade has replaced war as a nation's way to enrich itself.

14 Traded with Egypt and the Romans, as archaeological evidence points out. Indus Valley traded with Sumer.

The Hindu distaste for war and the preference for trade make the future full of opportunities.

The Indian was earlier at a disadvantage. Now that trade has become a dominant feature in the international arena, he should be at an advantage. The new phase of history offers us a golden opportunity. All we need today is to put our economic act together, achieve national synergy by a spirit of nationalism which, in turn, Hinduness can provide. We would be ready for a take-off in the Olympics of international trade.

Threat

The military has been a perennial blind spot of Indian civilisation. While Indian Muslim rulers like the Lodis and the Mughals suffered their share of defeats, as a generalisation, ability at warfare has been particularly a Hindu weakness. Although the lust for territory and the race for colonies withered by the end of World War II, war between nations is a continuing possibility. National interests, commercial or strategic, can clash and lead to war. Moreover, the collective ego of a country can lead to a flare up. In short, India must make sure that it is always militarily competent.

Let us take the Sino-Indian war of 1962 as an example. To blame only the fumbling generals and the blundering defence minister Krishna Menon is not sufficient. The ultimate responsibility must be borne by the then Prime Minister Jawaharlal Nehru. Had he kept his cool and consulted the right people even after initial setbacks, India could have come off honourably at least in the eastern sector. The invasion began on 20th October or at the beginning of autumn. This means that either the Chinese were not interested in a prolonged action or were prepared to spend the cold winter on the mountains of North East Frontier Agency (NEFA).

We were fully aware that most of our troops did not have the clothes for the cold in the mountains. Our artillery did not possess mountain guns that would fire at a high trajectory. The obvious answer therefore was to retreat to the plains of Assam and to remain relatively unscathed in order to meet the Chinese on a level fighting field. There would have been nothing novel about such a manoeuvre.

'Defence in depth' had already been theorised on the basis of how Field Marshal Erich von Manstein, a Wehrmacht commander, slowed down the Soviet invasion of central Europe by retreating faster and deeper than the Red Army could advance. Thereafter, his troops could cut off and surround the overextended Soviets from their flanks.

Over a century earlier, Carl von Clausewitz, the guru of conventional warfare, wrote a primer for the child crown prince of Prussia. In it, he wrote that one should never depend on the terrain. If the enemy cannot cross it, he would find a way of circumventing it. This is precisely what happened in 1962 when the Chinese bypassed the Sela Pass, whereas our generals waited for the enemy to cross it.

As it happened, the Chinese declared a unilateral ceasefire on the night of 20th November while Prime Minister Nehru was asleep. The Home Minister was unaware of the declaration even at 5.30 the next morning. Unaware, he arrived at Palam airport to catch a special plane to Assam in order to instruct that the oil wells there be rendered unusable if they were to fall into enemy hands. MC Bhatt, then secretary of Oil India Limited was to fly in the same plane. The Home Minister, on reading the newspapers, tried to phone the Prime Minister who was asleep. He then personally went to see the PM.

Many of us are aware of our military history and the catalogue of invasions suffered by India. It is, however, not widely realised that the last time we defeated and drove out an invader was in the 4th century BC when Chandragupta Maurya prevailed over the Greek Seleucus, whom Alexander the Great had left behind, when he retreated from India.

Defeating Pakistan, whether in 1971 or later, is like winning a civil war. Nor has our great civilisation been able to innovate a military weapon or technology of warfare. In fact, we did not learn lessons from a previous defeat, which explains why the invader won every time. This was not merely a Hindu failure. Ibrahim Lodi failed in 1526 as did Hemu at the Second Battle of Panipat in 1556 and as did Bhao Sahib, uncle of the Peshwa at the Third Battle of Panipat in 1761.

Before that, Nadir Shah humiliated the redoubtable Mughal emperor in 1739, burnt and looted Delhi. Amongst the booty he took back to Iran was the Peacock Throne and the Kohinoor diamond from the Red Fort at Shahjahanabad. His successor Ahmed Shah Abdali invaded India nine times between 1747 and 1761 and plundered Agra, Delhi, Mathura and Vrindavan at his sweet will. This is to emphasise that somehow we failed to learn the lessons of one defeat and moved on from one invasion to another without ever securing a victory.

It is uncanny that our civilisation did not record enough by way of history until the advent of the British. It is true that during the medieval period, badshahs and sultans commissioned their courtiers to write the chronicles of their reigns. Ancient India produced vast treasures of philosophical writings starting with the Rig Veda. A great deal of verse and drama were written. Sculpture, dance and music flourished. It is equally strange that to this day we have written very little political theory and even less by way of national strategy. Regardless of our preferences, we Indians must learn to change so that we can compete as well as deal successfully with other countries.

The Misconception of Fatalism

The Hindu ethos is frequently misunderstood as a credo that is intrinsically fatalistic. But the reality is that a Hindu cannot be considered a fatalist if only he understands the explanation of his faith or the basic tenets of Hinduism.

The spiritual basis of Western civilisation is provided by Judaic values, ie. there is an Almighty who is identifiable as an omniscient entity. The Jews call Him Jehova, the Christians God and Muslims Allah. All these religions are rooted in the lore of Abraham as the first father.

Socialism is nothing but the fourth sibling of the Judaic brotherhood. It is a natural continuity in the chain. A common fundamental presumption is that man came as an equal to this earth but society made men unequal. These religions have holy books, the Torah, the Bible, the Quran and *Das Kapital*; each believing in a single life. Marxism believes that the state will wither away as soon as an idyllic society has been established on earth. There will, thereafter, be bliss for all because all human beings will be equal. They cannot be divided between those rewarded with paradise and those committed to purgatory.

From each according to his ability, to each according to his need is the Marxist dictum of equality before the arrival of bliss. After that, it should perhaps be from each according to his sins, to each according to his paradise! There can be no other way to ensure equality. But the other three religions propagate the concept of doomsday which, in Islam, is called *qayaamat*, when the Almighty will sit on judgment over the conduct of people on earth and send them to heaven or hell according to what each person deserves.

The Hindu ethos has hardly anything in common with this Judaic belief. There is no concept of the Almighty or even a remotely identifiable entity. The collective soul of all living beings is called paramatma or the supreme soul. All the ordinary living beings, whether human, animal, bird or reptile, have a jeevatma or an individual soul. The endeavour of each individual should be to lead as good a life as possible in the hope of being able to reach the paramatma and, in the process, eventually not be reborn. That is called mukti or the Hindu view of salvation.

What is a good life is for the individual to decide and live.

There are guidelines, but no definite paths are prescribed. There is no overriding Holy Book; no concept of heaven. There is no doomsday or any day of judgment, nor is there a single life. The jeevatma continues to live until it reaches the paramatma. Life, as consciously experienced, is merely a continuum of incarnations with birth alternating death as punctuations from one stage to the other. In the Judaic ethos, each individual life is complete and ends with death. For the Hindu, a life is at best a stage in the journey towards mukti. Buddhism calls it *nirvana* while Jainism describes it as *moksha*.

Yet, Hinduism has been condemned as polytheistic whereas the Westerner has prided himself as a monotheist or a believer in one Almighty. In Hinduism, there is no Almighty. How can there be either a poly- or a mono-god? Yes, there are avatars or incarnations like Rama, Krishna, Buddha, Mahavir or Nanak.

What needs to be appreciated is that the avatars are super-souls or *atmas* who have earlier attained mukti, but have come back to the earth in order to save it from decline and to revive its quality. They can be called *muktatmas*. But they are not either Almighties or Gods. In the Christian idiom, they can perhaps be called apostles.

There are also *mahatmas*. Gandhi is considered one such great soul, rather like a saint in Christianity. All—whether jeevatma, mahatma, muktatma or paramatma—are ultimately one total soul. To that extent, all living beings are extensions of divinity. This then is the Hindu explanation, so very different from the Judaic belief.

As it happens, over the last few centuries, Western civilisation has flourished and more or less dominated the world. Inevitably, there has been a tendency to measure the whole world and all organisations with the Judaic yardstick. Anything different tends to be dismissed as inferior. Regrettably, there have not been many Hindu savants who have stood up and explained what Hinduism is. True, there was the great Swami Vivekananda who had an electrifying effect on some people in the West. Unfortunately, he passed away very young.

Then there was Sri Aurobindo who would not stir out of Pondicherry and go out of the country to explain Hinduism. Even then, many were spontaneously attracted to him and his philosophy. There were scholars like Sarvepalli Radhakrishnan who knew and could explain. They did so, but again to only a select audience. In the process, the average Westerner continued to believe in his superiority and tragically the average Indian accepted, even if implicitly, his inferiority.

A preoccupation with equality, which we have seen at the centre of the Judaic ethos, leads to social intervention. There is life at the end of which there is an assessment by the Almighty regarding performance in society. There is, therefore, no concept of *sanyas* or renouncement in the Judaic ethos. Atonement, yes; renouncement, no.

Social performance needs a mechanism or a network. One may call it organisation. The result is that societies of the West are organised. In sharp contrast, the Hindu society functions on the principle of liberty, as distinct from equality. There cannot be a ceiling on the good deeds a man might do. If there is no lid on karma, or deed, there can be no limit on bhagya or destiny.

Since there is no single life, there is no special hurry to perform socially. In any case, several of the paths recommended for an individual to work towards achieving mukti are unconnected with performance in society. For instance, bhakti is total devotion. Jnanayoga or the path of self realisation as pursued by Sri Aurobindo is oriented towards self-realisation.

When an organised society believing in equality and one life came in contact with a less organised milieu believing in liberty and continuity of birth, death and rebirth, the former did not understand the latter and assumed itself as the superior. Moreover, it was a case of the conqueror sitting in judgment over the conquered. It all seemed to the East as well as to the West that the Occident was superior and the Orient was inferior. Actually, it is karma or deed, which is the cause that results in bhagya or destiny; this is the essence of the Hindu faith. Cause and effect is a rational explanation. The issue of fatalism therefore, does not arise.

Tolerance in Hinduism

There can be any number of definitions of secularism. One is the separation of the church from the state. The second would be the abolition of the church as was attempted by communist states led by the Soviet Union. Yet a third one might be the Indian version; ideally, the equality of all religions before the state. The fourth would be the English variety whereby the state is formally a theocracy; the monarch is also the head of the Anglican Church. Yet, in practice, England is a just and liberal society.

The term secularism has its origin in the Reformation in 16th century Europe. The Reformation was not against religion or Christianity; it opposed the Catholic Church whose followers owed extraterritorial loyalty to the Pope. This allegiance to Rome resulted in the drain of wealth from other countries of Europe to Italy.

There were ad hoc contributions to be sent, for example, to build a new St Peter's cathedral in Rome. There were also regular levies like the tax on farm produce and cattle. It was estimated that every year some 300,000 gold coins found their way from Germany alone to Italy.

'Why should Germans put up with such extortion by Rome?' was a common question during the period of the Reformation. 'Why should not the German clergy establish a national church under the Archbishop of Mainz?' was another popular question. A German priest called Martin Luther planted his standard of revolt, not in religious terms but on the basis of the national spirit. Wherever nationalism won, the Reformation succeeded and the church became Protestant.

In France, the Reformation took a different turn. With tact and diplomacy, in 1516, King Francis took over from the Pope the powers to appoint the priests in his kingdom. It was said that the 'nationalisation of Christianity' was achieved in France without war or rebellion. The same could not be said for England where the instigating cause of the Reformation was King Henry VIII's desire for a son and heir. The story goes that since divorce was unthinkable for a Catholic in those times, he wanted his marriage to Queen Catherine annulled, as she had failed to give him a son. The Pope could not oblige as he was a virtual prisoner of Charles V, King of Spain and nephew of Queen Catherine.

England went to war with Spain but to no avail. Finally, on 3rd November 1529, King Henry called the parliament which abolished the right of the Pope to govern the church in England. The nationalist spirit was even stronger in England than in Germany. The priests did not like to make the king their spiritual head, but they considered the foreign influence of Pope to be a greater evil.

What came through from the history of the Reformation was the revulsion against and the rejection of the senior priests due to their extraterritorial loyalty, their greed and womanising. Doctrinal disputes were few; some in Germany; but none in England and France, for example. Even the radical views of

Martin Luther were not such as to require a complete break with Rome. There was a widespread demand to exclude the senior priests from interfering in the conduct of government, or at least, to make the bishops and abbots subordinate to the kings and princes.

In France, this was done by diplomacy and mutual understanding. In England, the monarch replaced the Pope as the head of the church and to this day, Britain is formally a theocracy. In Germany, the priests owing allegiance to Rome were replaced by those loyal to their own soil. The northern areas of Europe broke away as Protestants but the southern ones remained Catholic. There has not been much change in this regard since the 16th century.

This was the Reformation as a result of which the concept of secularism or anti-clericalism became Europe's political credo. It was not rejection of either religion or Christianity, nor a formal or deliberate separation of the church from the state. As we have seen in England, the church and the state were rolled into one in the office of the monarch.

Three centuries later, socialism emerged to be a standard bearer of secularism. Karl Marx had interpreted human history as the epic of class conflict whereby the powerful enriched themselves by taking away the wealth created by those who toiled. The toilers thus remained poor and their desire to reject their exploiters was blunted by the fear of God instilled into them by religion. That was the reason Marx dubbed religion the opium of the masses.

Communist states have treated this as a commandment. Beginning with the former Soviet Union and carried on in all such states, there was a systematic endeavour to abolish worship and the practice of traditional religion, whether Christianity or Islam or Judaism or Buddhism. Cathedrals, churches, mosques, synagogues and pagodas were closed down and the buildings converted into museums, libraries or government offices. If in every city or town one or two places of worship were left alone, it was for purposes of display or for reasons of diplomacy.

Marxist secularism was therefore not separation of the church from the state but total abolition of traditional religion from society. The communist credo was the denial of God and the enforcement of atheism.

Whether Marxist or Christian, secularism is essentially a European concept. It is difficult for any Asian scene to relate to it. In India, secularism has meant different things to different people. To anyone who is reasonable, it means the freedom of worship and the equality of all religious groups before the law. The state must be equidistant from all denominations. But for those seeking political or electoral advantage, it offers scope for manipulation. Secularism has been used to divide and divert the attention of the Hindus while some political parties pampered the *mullah*s (the Muslim clergy) and their agents. The 1987 Supreme Court judgment in the Shah Bano case was overturned by the Congress government, which passed the Muslim Women's Bill.

In Kerala, from time to time, the Congress as well as the Communist Party of India (Marxist) has formed coalition governments with the Muslim League. The pre-Independence League did not admit anyone as a member except a Muslim. It was the cause of India's partition. Yet, partnership with the League has never been condemned as anti-secular. There are countless instances of such double standards in the name of secularism. The word should better be avoided in India where 'religious tolerance' should be a preferred expression because it has been an integral feature of the Hindu world view.

Every Judaic or Abrahamic ethos conceptually divides humanity into 'us and them'. The Jews call the other Gentiles, Christians label non-Christians as heathens or pagans. The Muslim divided the universe into *momin*s and *kafir*s, whereas in Marxism the division is between the proletariat and the bourgeoisie. The Hindu ethos not only does not divide into 'us and them', but instead considers all living beings, be they human, animal, birds or reptiles, as part of one universe. This all inclusiveness is the foundation of Hindu tolerance.

Its philosophical superstructure is the belief in the transmigration of the souls amongst the various living beings. The soul is permanent, whereas the body is merely like clothes which are shed at death and new ones are acquired at birth. The individual souls or jeevatmas move from body to body when reborn. Religion is incidental to the parents of the child and is not a permanent attribute of the jeevatmas. Hence conceptually, there is no prejudice. Nor has there been any great inclination for Hindus to convert members of other faiths.

The corollary of transmigration is also the fear that the soul of one's own near and dear one, who died some time ago, might be resident in any body. This fear makes the Hindu comparatively reluctant to kill anyone. This is the conceptual basis whereby the Hindu prefers tolerance even towards animals, which, in turn, leads to his bias for vegetarian food.

Neither Fundamentalism nor Fascism

The word 'fundamentalism' was first used to describe the conservative Christian who referred to the Bible as his argument to resist Darwin's theory of evolution. This happened in Britain, Oxford to be more precise. Since Hinduism has nothing comparable to the Bible, its follower cannot be a fundamentalist. *The frequent use of the word fundamentalism in India is of recent origin. That was in the wake of Jarnail Singh Bhindranwale turning militant, around 1981.*

Indira Gandhi and, in fact, all her supporters had to find a *special word* to condemn him and his fellowmen. They could not use the word communal because, in their idiom, the expression was earmarked for the devotees of Hinduness. They promptly imported the word 'fundamentalist' from the USA.

The Americans had exhumed the word in order to abuse Ayatollah Khomeini who had thrown out Washington's puppet monarch Reza Shah Pahlavi from the throne of Iran. There is a reason why I have used the word exhumed. Fundamentalism had for decades been forgotten in the United States. It had come into prominence after World War I and, after a few years, had fallen into disuse.

The theory of evolution by Charles Darwin had crossed the Atlantic and gained currency in the USA. Many people, including the liberal among the priests, began to appreciate Darwin's contention. His great work, on the origin of species by means of natural selection, or the preservation of favoured races in the struggle for life had been published in England in 1859. A storm of protest soon arose over the book, reaching its height at Oxford in 1860 when a scientist called TH Huxley and Bishop Wilberforce fought a gun duel. The acceptance of the new theory threatened to pull the carpet from under the Biblical doctrine of creation.

It was a challenge to religion by science. The Christian belief was that God created the world in six days. On the first day the heavens and the earth were created. Then came light, which led to the split between day and night. Then the earth's surface was divided between land and sea. Then came herbs and fruits, followed by sea monsters, reptiles and animals. Then came man and woman. And so on, until the seventh day when God rested.

In 1923, the General Assembly of the Presbyterian Church in the USA reasserted the five points which were the pillars of the Christian faith: the virgin birth of Christ, his physical resurrection, the inerrancy of the Scripture or Bible, the substitutionary Atonement and belief in the miracles. The Assembly reprimanded the New York Presbyter for licensing a student who refused to affirm virgin birth.

In 1925, a teacher of science in Dayton, Tennessee named John T Scopes was tried and fined a hundred dollars for teaching Darwin's theory of evolution. The origin of the word fundamentalism therefore, related to a dispute between Christian conservatives and the liberals. The former were called fundamentalists by the latter. The liberals had the proof of scientific discovery on their side. The only way the conservatives could defend or conserve their viewpoint was an appeal to the fundamentals which were ordained by the Holy Book.

A Muslim can be a fundamentalist. Anyone who denounces change but cannot argue against it on the basis of reason or merit is vulnerable to the charge of being a fundamentalist because he takes shelter under what is written in the Holy Quran or the Hadith. This does not denote anything derogatory but is a fact because he or she abides by the fundamental.

On the other hand, a Hindu can be a bigot but he cannot appeal to or insist on a fundamental. Hinduism or the *Sanatan Dharma* is *anadi-anant* or one without a beginning and without an end. It has no comprehensive code or final message or scripture, no single book, nor a founder or a prophet.

Explaining Fascism

Fascism is an eco-political ideology which stands for class collaboration as distinct from capitalism as well as communism. The former has been traditionally identified with class exploitation and the latter with class conflict. In contrast, fascism attempted to combine the effort of all classes. Professor Alfredo Rocco, the Minister of Justice in the Mussolini cabinet, set forth the gist of this new ideology in the course of a speech at Perugia in 1925. According to him, *society does not exist for the individual, but the individual exists for society; economic progress is a social interest and all classes of people should collaborate to maximise production. He held the interests of employers and the employees to be identical. To ensure that this was practised, there was a system of state discipline over class conflicts.* Strikes and lockouts were both illegal and punishable by heavy fines and imprisonment.

Wherever possible, employers and workers in each industry, trade or profession were organised together in syndic associations. Wherever it was not possible to form such syndicates, the unions' and the employers' associations remained but combined to form guilds to ensure coordination. If collective bargaining did not prove satisfactory, the disputes were referred to law courts. This is how class collaboration was conceptualised by the Fascist Party. In practice, the economy was toned up by rearmament and public works. Soldiers and workers in large numbers were recruited in factories to produce arms. This would bring profits to the bourgeoisie who could then pay the proletariat well. Urban prosperity would increase demand for agricultural produce. What was left of the unemployed youth was absorbed by the armed forces. The promise to the whole nation was foreign conquests which would bring booty. The Albanian adventure and the invasion of Abyssinia were two efforts to fulfil this promise until, of course, World War II broke out.

Another example of the practice of fascist class collaboration, albeit on a much more limited scale, was in Spain under General Franco. Neither the Italian nor the Spanish experience is known in any great detail in India. What, however, the members of the intelligentsia are familiar with are the exploits of Adolf Hitler and his Nazi Party whose full name was National Socialist German Workingmen's Party. It was founded by Hitler and his six comrades in Munich in 1920. The economic deprivation in Germany was much greater than witnessed in Italy. The country paid an exorbitant price for its defeat in World War I. The runaway inflation as well as the global depression caused by the 1929 Wall Street stock market crash made matters worse. It was then widely believed that Hitler's programme of class collaboration saved Germany from utter collapse and a communist takeover.

Nazism is known more for its violence than for its ideology. *However, as a theory, fascism is as neutral to violence as any other.* Stalin's Soviet Union had its orgies of violence.

Even a democratic North America took a heavy toll of the lives of Red Indians; virtually wiped them out of existence. Indira Gandhi's Emergency also walked on the apron of state violence before it got snuffed out by the 1977 general election.

The Medieval Phase

Traumatised by invasions, Hinduism survived with the help of its bhakti saints who took the spirit of the faith to the masses.[15] Shivaji waged a struggle for Hindu revival. During the medieval period, the cause was pursued socio-religiously through a galaxy of saints. They played a yeoman role in integrating the caste-ridden Hindu society. They helped to transfer the Hindu ethos from the philosophical to the devotional, from the intellectual to the popular, from the meditational to the mystical level. The benefits of the culture were distributed widely from the portal of the learned to the hutment of the commoner.

Ramanuja was the leading one among the Vaishnava

15 The 'bhakti' phenomenon arose simultaneously with Adi Sankara's revivalism. In the South of India, with the Alvar saints like Andal in 8th Century AD and Akka Mahadevi (1130-1160) who first sang of Vishnu bhakti and Shiva bhakti, devotion, and from hereon expanded the 'devotional' nontheocratic cult in Hinduism. In 1377 came Nundrishi of Kashmir, Islam co-opting bhakti to emerge as the 'sufi'.

mystics. He died in 1137 AD. Madhva was a Kannada Brahmin who founded a sect known by his name in the following century. About the same time, the Telugu Brahmin Nimbarka settled near Mathura to sing the praises of Krishna.

In Maharashtra, between 1271 and 1296 AD, Jnaneshwara wrote the *Bhavarthadipika*, or a commentary on the Bhagwad Gita, which proved to be the fountainhead of devotionalism in this region. Namdev, 1270 to 1350 AD, was a tailor by caste who took to the bhakti of Vithoba, an incarnation of Vishnu, at the still popular temple at Pandharpur. He was surrounded by several holy men who had, like him, humble origins. Among them were Gora the potter, Samvata the gardener, Chokha the untouchable, Sena the barber and Janabai the maid.

Two centuries later came Eknath who revived the bhakti tradition in Maharashtra. He gave the people a popular commentary on the Ramayana. Above all, he showed how every Hindu could aspire to the deepest religious experience no matter how many obstacles the Muslims put in his way, for example by razing temples to the ground as had been done to the one at Pandharpur.

As is well known, Tukaram, 1598 to 1650 AD, was an outstanding bhakti poet from Maharashtra. Ramdas (1608 to 1681 AD), orphaned as a child, left home and, after long years of spiritual training and wandering, settled down on the banks of the river Krishna where he built temples of Shri Rama. The threat of Islam was on his mind. He, therefore, stood for activism. Shivaji, the great Maratha ruler, was his pupil.

In Bengal, devotionalism had several inspirations; the Vaishnava impetus began with Jayadeva and his *Gitagovinda*. Chandidas, in the fourteenth century was an unforgettable name in bhakti literature. Then came the even more famous and revered Chaitanya who lived, sang, danced and reformed between 1485 and 1533 AD.The Assamese practiced Tantricism before Shankardeva (1449-1568) and Madhavdev (1489–1596) brought the Vaishnavite faith into the Brahmaputra islands. This 15th century form of worship is practiced even today.

The Hindi heartland also produced its galaxy of *bhakta*s or distinguished devotees. Ram was the popular avatar, unlike other areas where Krishna inspired more bhakti. Ramananda (1400-1470 AD) was the first of the distinguished bhaktas followed by Kabir who was four decades his junior, Tulsidas was the other famous spiritual heir of Ramananda and a contemporary of Akbar, the Mughal emperor. He wrote the *Ramcharitmanas* which was the Ramayana in Hindi instead of the original Sanskrit by Valmiki. Guru Nanak (1469-1539) created a distinctly egalitarian stream of belief and gave the foreword for the textual basis of the stream, the *Adi Granth* (1560-1600s).

This mystic outburst across north India led to the growth of the popular languages—later called vernaculars by the British—to distinguish them from the classical Sanskrit, Pali or Ardhamagadhi.

As the epics were translated or rewritten as for example, the 12th century *Gitagovinda,* Tulsidas' *Ramcharitmanas*, Rahim's dohas on Radha Krishna (during Akbar's time again), literature flourished in prose as well as poetry. Countless bhajans or devotional songs from the likes of Meerabai (1498-1557 when Babar was trying to conquer India) fertilised both verse and music. The blind Surdas, who lived between 1483 and 1563 AD, also expressed his devotion through song and music.

Shankaradeva in Assamese, Chandidas in Bengali, Vidyapati in Maithili, Narsi Mehta in Gujarati, Mirabai in Rajasthani, Kabir in Bhojpuri-cum-Urdu, Surdas in Brajbhasha, Namdev and Eknath in Marathi, Saraladas in

Oriya and above all, Guru Nanak in Punjabi contributed not only to bhakti but also to the popular languages and literature.

'Why should we remain content with what the Muslim rulers choose to give us? We are Hindus. This whole country is ours by right, and is yet occupied and held by foreigners. They desecrate our temples, break holy idols, plunder our wealth, convert us forcibly to their religion, carry away our womenfolk and children, slay the cows and inflict a thousand wrongs upon us. We will suffer this treatment no more. We possess strength in our arms. Let us draw the sword in defence of our sacred religion, liberate our country. Are we not as brave and capable as our ancestors of yore? Let us undertake this holy mission and God will surely help us. We are the captains of our fortunes and the makers of our freedom', said Shivaji.

A close look at Shivaji's life reveals his intense regard for Hinduism. He cared more about emancipation of his land than mere political dominion. The religious persecution practised by Bijapur and the Mughals moved Shivaji intensely and influenced his actions. At the same time, he realised that religious freedom could not be obtained without political power, and to that extent, he exerted himself in freeing his homeland from Muslim control. As a result of his visit to Aurangzeb's court, he was perhaps convinced of the hollowness of the Mughal empire, and thereafter exerted himself in bringing India under Hindu control. The imposition of *chauth* or one fourth revenue on lands outside his immediate sway was a means to that end. His coronation ceremony and the grand title of *Chhatrapati* he assumed point to his intention of establishing a Hindu empire.

Shivaji's expedition to Karnataka was a clear move towards a Hindu India in which pursuit he roped in Qutab Shah of Hyderabad. If he had been gifted with a little longer span of life, he might have brought about the deposition of Aurangzeb, so clearly emphasised a little later by his son Sambhaji in his Sanskrit letter to Ram Singh. That Hindustan is essentially a land of the Hindus, and other similar phrases scattered throughout Sanskrit and Marathi literature are sentiments actuated by Shivaji's endeavour so closely followed after him by the Peshwas. Mahadji Sindhia indeed felt the glory of having achieved some of these dreams when he attained supreme power at the court of Delhi. The Peshwas, over several generations, carried the Hindu *bhagwa* or saffron flag far and wide, as did the other Maratha families like the Scindias, the Holkars and the Gaekwads. The territories they captured ranged from Delhi in the north to Karnataka in the south; from Bengal in the east to Gujarat in the west.

Hindu Resurgence in the 19th Century

Hindu renaissance began with the advent of British intervention. As we know, the word 'Hindutva' in the 19th century was given by Rajnarain Bose, who along with Nabagopal Mitra, in 1886 started the Hindu Mela. The latter also set up gymnasia that became training schools in martial arts teaching Bengali young men to wield the *lathi*, dagger and sword. The wealthy zamindar Debendranath Tagore, father of Gurudev Rabindranath, lent his support to the Hindu Mela.

Swamy Dayanand's outstanding contribution was the revival, *shuddhi*. This was an ancient Hindu method of purifying any Hindu, who got polluted. For instance, crossing the ocean of black waters or the seas was often considered a cause of pollution. The second use of shuddhi was for the reinstatement of a lapsed Hindu like someone who, or whose ancestor, had got converted say, to a religion of the Book. During the medieval period or the dark age of Hinduism, this ancient custom was forgotten. The Atharva Veda prescribed the rite *vratyastoma* for *readmitting* those who had fallen beyond the pale of society.

Bankim Chandra Chatterji, with his epoch novel *Anand Math* in 1882, provided the next milestone for those marching on the road of Hindutva. *Vande Mataram* overnight became the anthem of Hinduness. Many a sentence contained in *Anand Math* epitomised the essence of nationalism: 'He (the child) alone is worthy of this duty who has renounced everything for the sake of Mother India. The man whose heart is tied with the string of human attachment is like a kite tied to the reel; it cannot fly high or far from the earth below.' 'Splendid! Do you both renounce your castes? For all children belong to the same caste, in our work there is no Hindu or Muslim, Buddhist or Sikh or Parsee. We are all brothers here––all children of the same Mother India.' 'I want to tell you that this country belongs to us. This is our motherland. Why don't you Englishmen, like true Christians, return peacefully to your homeland?' 'I have addressed only my Mother India as mother. I can never allow myself to cause my husband to leave his path of duty. If my husband has to die at your command, let him die. I can never, never ask him not to die', says a protagonist in *Anand Math*.

Swami Vivekananda awoke the interested Western world to the wisdom that is Hinduism. This perennial explanation of the mysteries of life on earth was unknown to almost everyone in Europe and America. Vivekananda burst upon the world in 1893 at the Parliament of Religions held at Chicago, laying the foundation of acquiring legitimacy for Hinduness in the eyes of the world. That was the third milestone. If only we all can now communicate half as well as he did, single-handed in a matter of a few years, Hinduness may well become the world's dominant ideology. To quote a few of Vivekananda's sentences:

> The one common ground that we have is our sacred tradition, our religion...in Europe, political ideas form the national unity. In Asia, religious ideals do so. Unity in religion, therefore, is absolutely necessary as the first condition of the future of India. What do I mean by one religion? Not

> in the sense of one religion as held among the Christians, or the Mohammedans, or the Buddhists. There are certain common grounds; and within their limitations this religion of ours admits of a marvelous variation, an infinite amount of liberty to think and live our own lives.
>
> We see how in Asia, especially in India, race difficulties, linguistic difficulties, social difficulties and national difficulties, all melt away before this unifying power of religion. We know that to the Indian mind there is nothing higher than religion's ideals, that this is the keynote of Indian life...it is the only possible means of work; work in any other line, without first strengthening this, would be disastrous. Therefore the first plank in the making of a future India, the first step that is to be hewn out of that rock of ages, is this unification of religion.
>
> We have seen that our vigour, our strength, nay our national life, is in our religion...you have withstood the shocks of centuries simply because you took great care of it. You sacrificed everything else for it. Your forefathers underwent everything boldly, even death itself, but preserved their religion. Temple after temple was broken down by the foreign conqueror, but no sooner had the wave passed than the spire of the temple rose up again. Some of these old temples of southern India and those like Somnath of Gujarat will teach you volumes of wisdom, will give you a keener insight into the history of the race than any amount of books. Mark how these temples bear the mark of a hundred attacks and a hundred regenerations, continually destroyed and continually springing up from the ruin rejuvenated and strong as ever.

Sri Aurobindo was another sage whose thinking has enriched the philosophy of Hinduness. In 1907, he wrote:

> Swami Dayanand awoke to the need for re-introducing shuddhi at Calcutta, which he visited in 1872, perhaps as a

> result of his contact with Brahmo Samaj leaders like Keshub Chandra Sen. Dayanand's contribution to Hinduness was monumental. We must remember that the overwhelming majority of Christians and Muslims in our country are lapsed Hindus. It is quite possible that some of them may wish to return to the Hindu fold. How can anyone be welcomed unless there is a gateway? It was Dayanand who reopened the gate that had been shut and forgotten for centuries.
>
> Nationalism depends for its success on the awakening and organising of the whole strength of the nation: it is, therefore, vitally important. Nationalism can awaken the politically backward classes and bring into the current of political life, the great mass of our people.

In 1908, he wrote:

> The new nationalism overleaps every barrier; it calls to the clerk at his counter, the trader in his shop, the peasant at his plough; it summons the Brahmin from his temple and takes the hand of the Chandala in his degradation; it seeks out the student in his college, the schoolboy at his book, it touches the very child in its mother's arms; and the secluded *zenana* has thrilled to its voice; its eyes searches the jungle for the Santhal and travels the hills for the wild tribes of the mountains. It cares nothing for age or sex or caste or wealth or education or respectability; it mocks at the talk of a stake in the country; it spurns aside the demand for a property qualification or a certificate of literacy. It speaks to the illiterate or the man in the street in such vigorous language as he best understands. It cries to all to come forth, to help in God's work and remake a nation, each with what his creed or his culture, his strength, his manhood or his genius can give to the new nationality. The only qualification it asks for is a body made in the womb of an Indian mother,

> a heart that can feel for India, a brain that can think and plan for her greatness, a tongue that can adore her name, of hands that can fight in her quarrel. The new nationalism is the rebirth of India of the Kshatriya, the samurai.

In 1909, he wrote:

> An Indian nationalism, largely Hindu in its spirit and traditions, because the Hindu made the land and the people and persists, by the greatness of his past, his civilisation and his culture and his invincible virility.

In 1926, Sri Aurobindo wrote:

> Did India have the national idea in the modern sense? The 'Nation Idea' India never had. By that I mean the political idea of the nation. It is a modern growth. But we had in India the cultural and spiritual idea of the nation.

Bal Gangadhar Tilak is most remembered for his proclaiming: 'Swaraj is my birthright'. He had, according to Parshotam Mehra, professor of history at the Punjab University, a profound respect for Hindu tradition, religion, philosophy and ethics. The *Gita Rahasya* is a monument to his scholarship. But he did not merely comment on the Gita; he lived it. Tilak tried to arouse national pride and Hindu unity by revitalising well known religious festivals, and resurrecting forgotten national heroes. It was thus in 1893 he revived the Ganapati festival and two years later the Shivaji festival. He later refuted the charge that his propagation of these celebrations had any anti-Muslim inspiration. His prime motive was to unite all Indians.

Veer Savarkar's magnum opus *Hindutva* was the first serious effort to define this concept of cultural nationalism. The book was published first in 1923 when Savarkar was in the Ratnagiri jail. Its authorship was therefore ascribed to 'A Maratha'. The ideas, however, were formed over the many years since 1906 when he was studying law in England. A Hindu, according to Vinayak Damodar Savarkar, is anyone who acknowledges Hindustan as his fatherland or *pitribhu* as well as his holy land, *punyabhu*. Whether he or she is a devotee of *sanatan dharma* is unimportant, anyone who himself or his ancestor was born in undivided India and who is even a Buddhist, whomsoever's ancestor was a Hindu but was converted to, say, Islam or Christianity is also welcome back to the Hindu fold, provided he accepts India as his fatherland-cum-holy land.

Hindutva is not a word but a history. Hinduism is only a derivative, a fraction or a part of Hindutva or Hinduness. Common blood, common culture, common customs and laws, common history all add up to Hindutva, according to Savarkar. His exercise in definition was novel and well thought out. It was an intellectual effort and influenced by the European ideas and idioms of his day.

To that extent, Savarkar's thinking was not as deeply rooted in Indian soil as that of Swami Vivekananda who felt that Asians proceed from religion to politics, unlike the Euro-Americans the other way about. To us, India is mother and not father. Fatherland is a German and Russian idiom.

Muslims—More than Equal Citizens?

What was wrong if, in the course of the *Gaurav Yatra* in Gujarat, it was pointed out by the then Chief Minister, Narendra Modi, that some people do not subscribe to family planning?

Whether self-styled secularists like to accept it or not, there is a deep-seated resentment among the Hindus against the double standards being practised. Lately, the exhortations to them are to limit themselves to one child, a la China. Earlier, it was *hum do, hamare do*. On the other hand, the Muslim Personal Law permits the keeping of four wives at any one time and an unlimited number over a man's lifetime. Modi exclaimed that some citizens could be *hum panch, hamare pachchees!* A law that can enable a husband to divorce any of his wives at the call of the word *talaq* three times is indeed pernicious. It has the potential of becoming: *hum ek, beevian anek aur bachchay beshumar* (many wives and unaccounted for offsprings). There is nothing new about this. The crowning insult heaped on Hindus in the name of secularism till date has perhaps been former Prime Minister Manmohan Singh's blatant appeal for Muslims to be accorded first right to the country's resources. Manmohan Singh went to the extent of issuing a clarion call of 'Muslims first.'[16]

BR Ambedkar as Law Minister in 1948 on the floor of the Constituent Assembly had pointed out that all the spheres of law, like criminal procedure, evidence, contract etc. had been made uniform. The only exceptions were the laws of marriage and succession. These were the two issues for a Uniform Civil Code not being accepted. Its idea was kept alive by a common code being a Directive Principle of Policy as Article 44 of the Constitution. Until 1937, the Muslims of India followed different traditions; many of them in UP, NWFP, Bombay State and CP were governed by the Hindu law of succession.

Soon after the Hindu Code Bill or the Special Marriages Act was passed in 1954, Prime Minister Nehru was asked about a uniform code. He told Parliament: 'Well, I would like a civil code which applies to everybody but wisdom hinders. If he (the member) or anybody else brings forward a Civil Code Bill, it will have my extreme sympathy. But I confess I do not think that at the present moment the time is ripe in India for me to try to push it through. I want to prepare the ground for it'. Unfortunately, ever since, none of the governments have had the courage to implement this Directive Principle of Policy.

Syed Shahbuddin, (4 November 1935-4 March 2017) an Indian politician and diplomat, in an article in *The Pioneer* (16.09.2002) stated: 'Our religious identity is basic to our cause. In fact, the very *raison d'être* of the Muslim Indians' struggle for survival and empowerment in the land of their birth is to preserve their religious identity and not to accept a

16 PTI | 9 Dec 2006, 06.28 pm IST.

tradeoff between identity and development.' The question is why should the whole country be hostage to the whims of a few or even a whole community?

It is not widely realised that minorityism is a violation of the Indian Constitution. Articles 14, 15 and 16 are part of the chapter on fundamental rights. Equality before the law is one such right. Article 14 says: 'The State shall not deny to any person equality before the law. Article 15 elucidates this fundamental stating that the State shall not discriminate against any citizen on grounds of religion, sex etc'.

The absence of a Uniform Civil Code allows a section of the Indian people to have four spouses. Without arguing for polygamy, polygamy for some and compulsory monogamy for others violates Article 15 of the Indian Constitution.

Even within the practice of Muslim Personal Law, there is blatant discrimination between the man and woman. A man is allowed to have four wives at any given point of time. He can divorce any or all the wives by uttering the word talaq three times.[17] On the other hand, the woman is not allowed more than one husband at a time. Nor is the facility of an instant divorce extended to her. She is permitted to pursue the process of *khul* if she wishes to take the initiative and seek separation from her husband. Are these not pernicious violations of a basic human right, not to speak of the flagrant disobedience of Article 15 of the Indian Constitution? It should not be forgotten that the Muslim woman is not allowed to pray in a masjid although, ironically, a non-Muslim man can walk into any masjid at any time.

Backwardness is Own Choice

Many a Muslim leader is heard to claim that his co-religionists constitute India's most backward community in all respects,

17 India is in the process of enacing legislation to end instant verbal triple talaq.

and therefore, should be given reservations in line with Scheduled Castes and Tribes.[18] This is just short of sacrilege. It is an insult to Muslims who were, lest it be forgotten, rulers of large tracts of Hindustan not so long ago. The Mughal emperor was acknowledged as India's temporal head and even the Marathas minted a coin in his name. In fact, Hindustan was recognised as Dar-ul-Islam on the strength of the Mughal empire's sway.

The kindest sentiment we have heard from our Muslim brethren is that their community should be considerate to Hindus who offered their ancestral space in a hospitable country. Hindus, they add, allowed Muslims to rule and gave a quarter of the country in 1947. Although Partition was demanded to give the Muslims a homeland, Hindus did not ask the Muslims to leave Hindustan. Nor did they create conditions whereby the latter would be forced to leave. Finally, our friends say, the Constitution, especially Articles 29 and 30 are favourable to the minority. On the other hand, the unkindest that we have heard Muslims say is that the Hindus are weak-willed cowards; that 'even ten of them are not equal to one of us'. Muslims thus reduce themselves to virtually begging for pity, sympathy and, of course, reservation.

They forget quota is rather like a handicap given to weaker players. Adivasis and the Dalits were denied the opportunities accorded to the upper castes, whether the rulers were Hindu, Muslim or British. Since Muslims ruled large tracts of the country for long centuries in the last millennium, perhaps they were as much responsible as the Hindu upper castes for the backwardness of these sections. Despite being the dominant

---

18 2006 Sachar Committee Report on Status of Muslims. https://timesofindia.indiatimes.com/city/nashik/Muslims-organisations-present-charter-of-demands-seeking-reservation-in-education-jobs/articleshow/55906064.cms

rulers, if Muslims are backward or less educated today, the blame must be borne by the Ashrafs or the privileged layer.

The Islamic brotherhood believes in the equality of all Muslims before Allah. One of the ways of equalising the well-to-do and others has been the institution of *zakat*, whereby a percentage of one's wealth is annually donated. It would flow that either a great deal of the zakat has not been paid or funds have been misdirected. Another instrument of redistribution and welfare is the *wakf* or the properties handed over to Allah for the benefit of the poor. Today these wakfs are reputed to be the largest urban landlords in India. Why then are the Muslims backward and less educated? Is it because wakf property is being misused by the *mutawalli*s or is it that the ulema are discouraging Muslim youth from pursuing secular studies?

The lesser a person's education, the greater his chances of not being given to thinking. With the advent of the British, the ulema had repeatedly appealed against Muslims learning English. Alien studies, according to it, would deviate the momin or the faithful from his path. How else can one explain the diversion of petrodollars for the building of masjids and madrasas instead of promoting career-oriented education?

Articles 29 and 30 delineate subsidising of education overseen by minority institutions at the nation's cost. As for Hajj subsidy, Indian Muslims' financial gain as a result of the subsidy is the nation's loss at the cost of the country.[19] Expenditure on sustaining Articles 29 and 30 itself runs into thousands of crores, whether paid out of the central or the state exchequers. Even after all this, Muslims ask for more, and in the process, they humiliate themselves.

---

19 Recent reports said the airline gets around Rs 700 crore annually from the government for the services. The subsidy given to Muslims for Haj, has been removed by the Narendra Modi government in 2017.
http://www.hindustantimes.com/mumbai-news/why-muslims-want-changes-in-haj-subsidy/story-0f0GPHrJmkAmyoiBk064iI.html

The Muslim does not know the Hindu well enough to be able to arrive at an ongoing cordiality based on a sympathetic understanding of one another. The Hindu knows his Muslim compatriot even less. They have seldom lived together, broken bread together or have spontaneously belonged to the same nation.

Many believe that the Hindu and the Muslim are separate nations. Partition took place on this belief. Nearly all the Hindus disagreed with the theory and therefore paid no heed to Qaid-e-Azam Jinnah's demand for an exchange of population whereby all the Muslims would settle in Pakistan and all the others should live in Hindustan.

Most Muslims on the Indian side of the border did not move and remained here. Yet many of them looked to Pakistan as the homeland; they stayed back because they had to. Although their bodies became Indian citizens, yet their souls yearned for the newly carved out Dar-ul-Islam. The breakup of Pakistan in 1971 shook them out of their implicit faith that Islam could be the basis of a country. The longing for the homeland weakened although their liking for the motherland did not increase.

The very mention of motherland irritates some Muslims. The disavowal of the anthem *Vande Mataram* reflects this sentiment. Islam is primarily a man's religion; the place of the woman is inferior. For example, two women witnesses equal one male witness in a court of law. Secondly, any hint of worship towards anyone other than Allah the merciful is sacrilege. To sing in obeisance to the motherland and to compare her with a goddess appears unbecoming to many a Muslim. A red *tika* on the forehead or the breaking of a coconut to inaugurate a function are always frowned upon. For a Muslim, they are symbolic of *another* religious tradition.

The Unfinished Agenda of Partition

Many questions were raised in response to the 23rd March

1940 resolution of the Muslim League for the creation of Pakistan. One of the most important was: no matter where the line of demarcation was drawn, there would be Hindus, Muslims and Sikhs on either side in a minority. They would overnight become aliens and foreigners in their own homes. Mohammed Ali Jinnah initially evaded this question, but later began to promise protection to the minorities. However, there was no question of Hindus and Sikhs obtaining citizenship or equal status with the nationals of Pakistan. If they could, why divide India was his question. Not satisfied himself with his own logic, he suggested an exchange of population as the realistic solution.

As if to avoid shocking people, Jinnah was slow and gentle in bringing up the question of population transfer. But wise and educated as he was, it is fair to believe that he was familiar with the European experience where, at the beginning of the 20th century, some two and a half million people had undertaken transfer of residence across national frontiers. Muslim Bulgarians were resettled in Turkey and many Turks were transferred to Bulgaria in pursuance of the Turko-Bulgarian Convention of 1913. This was also done officially under the Treaty of Lausanne signed on 30th January 1923 between Turkey and Greece. Professor M Mujeeb, Vice-Chancellor of Jamia Millia Islamia, New Delhi had an interesting experience. In his words, quoted from his book *Islamic Influence on Indian Society*, (Meenakshi Prakashan, Meerut, 1972): 'At a party given during the UN General Assembly Session in 1949 I had the pleasure of being placed next to the Turkish representative. He looked at my name card, saw that I was a Muslim and at once asked, are there still any Muslims in India? The impression then created does not yet seem to have been removed and it is believed that the sub-continent had been divided between Muslims and Hindus, with all Muslims on the one side and all Hindus on the other.'

Jinnah must surely have been aware of the philosophical mainspring of Pakistan. Ever since the British captured power and the consequent displacement of Muslim rule, there was widespread feeling that Dar-ul-Islam in India had been replaced by a Dar-ul-Harb or a land of war. There is a principle as old as Islam that *jihad* has to be fought for acquiring a Dar-ul-Islam. On the other hand, when there is no hope of achieving it, a Dar-ul-Harb cannot be tolerated indefinitely. The solution for the Muslims then was hijrat or migration to a land of Islam. Incidentally, devout faithful believe that they were fighting a jihad against the British right through the 19th century. Hijrat was also undertaken by several hundred thousand Muslims who migrated to Afghanistan in 1920 when they realised that the British would not allow the Sultan to continue on the throne of Turkey and thus remain the Khalifa for all Sunnis. Nearly 20,000 Indian Muslims entered and settled in Afghanistan.

It was implicit in these statements that the League objective was to undertake ethnic cleansing soon after partition. That this was not mere conjecture was proved by the fact that almost all Hindus were driven out from West Pakistan in a matter of two to three years. Evidently, the League leadership had fears that ethnic cleansing on their side would invite a similar action in Hindustan, causing untold miseries to their Muslim brethren. In any case, the Dar-ul-Islam that they were pursuing was for all Muslims of the subcontinent. Why should those, who happened to be in Hindustan, be condemned to live indefinitely in a hopeless Dar-ul-Harb?

These were no stray threats either by the *Mamdot* or the *Pir*. Jinnah, while addressing a press conference at Karachi on 25th November 1946, said that the authorities, both central and provincial, should immediately take up the question of exchange of population, as reported by *Dawn*, on 26th November 1946. Sir Feroze Khan Noon threatened to re-enact the murderous orgies of Genghis Khan and Halaqu

Khan Ismail Chundrigar, who also eventually rose to be Prime Minister of Pakistan, had said that the British had no right to hand over Muslims to a subject people over whom they had ruled for 500 years. Mohammad Ismail, a leader from Madras, had declared that the Muslims of India were in the midst of a jihad. Shaukat Hayat Khan, son of the Prime Minister of Punjab, Sir Sikander Hayat Khan, had threatened, while the British were still in India, of a rehearsal of what the Muslims would do to the Hindus eventually. *The point that came through clearly was that transfer of population was an integral part of the demand for Pakistan.*

What the politicians said was confirmed by Prof Mujeeb, in his erudite work. He said that the Muslim League demanded the creation of a separate homeland for Indian Muslims. He further stated that in the elections held early in 1946, the League, whose dominant manifesto was the creation of Pakistan, secured 425 seats out of 492 reserved for Muslims. The League insisted that the right to a separate homeland should be conceded first and all other negotiations could be held thereafter. He went on to say:

> The decision in regard to exchange of populations applied only to eastern and western Punjab. A large proportion of the Hindus in the North West Frontier Province and in Sind would have stayed on if they could. On the other hand, there would have been much less of immigration of the Hindus of East Pakistan into West Bengal and anti-Muslim sentiment in eastern and northern India would not have been constantly revived.

These ideas were no doubt repulsive to the Hindu, but it has to be admitted that the Muslim League leaders had a clear vision. Their demand for not only partition but also population transfer might have seemed abhorrent, but the fact was that the Muslim leadership had thought through the implications of carving out Pakistan. *If a division was to be made, it had to be thorough and comprehensive.*

It is the Congress leadership that faltered in thought and floundered in action. It would have been a different matter if they had not conceded partition. But having agreed to the division quite clearly on the basis of the two-nation theory propounded by the League, they had no right to be confused over its consequences. If they were unable to visualise what was to follow, they had every opportunity to consult the Hindu leaders of east Bengal and Hindu and Sikh leaders of Punjab, Sind and North West Frontier Province. But those who were likely to be affected the most were ignored. This makes the blundering by Congress leaders unforgivable.

Uncannily, once Jinnah took over leadership of the Muslims, the initiative was held by the League with the Congress being continually on the defensive. Nevertheless, the Congress did not even react. However ill-conceived partition might have seemed to many a Hindu as well as to a number of Muslim leaders like Maulana Abul Kalam Azad and Khan Abdul Ghaffar Khan, the fact was that Jinnah achieved it on his own terms.

The Hindu-Muslim Gulf

In their heart of hearts Hindus have grown up to hate Muslims. At the same time, by and large Muslims do not hate but certainly harbour contempt for the Hindus. This mutually antagonistic attitude has reflected the Hindu-Muslim equation right through the centuries, until the British began to assume power in India. Until then, the Muslim was the ruler and the Hindu, the subject across large tracts of the country. No doubt, there was a phase when the Marathas gained influence in many parts of India, but their domination was neither permanent nor widespread enough to correct the Hindu-Muslim imbalance that had grown over the centuries. This imbalance explains why there is no record of communal riots until after 1858 when the British crown directly assumed governance. How can there be a riot between a ruler and his fearful subjects? Riots can only take place when there is a semblance of balance.

The advent of the British signalled the defeat of those princes who were in power. Much more of India was ruled by Muslim nawabs than by Hindu rajas. The Mughal emperor was the titular head of the country; even the Marathas acknowledged him as such. The defeat was complete and formal when the rebellion or Mutiny of 1857 failed. As the British became rulers, Muslims as well as Hindus became subjects. Thus equality between the two communities was established for the first time. For the Hindus, it was a great relief that they had ceased to be either dhimmis or jaziya[20] payers. The British rulers were impartial umpires between the two communities.

These are facts. Yet, the myth of 'divide and rule' was created. Evidently, neither British scholars nor rulers were able to nip it in the bud. They certainly could not have relished being accused of such an unscrupulous policy. This indicates that there is yet another myth: that our history has been written with bias, only because the British had it written while they ruled the country. They did intervene and favoured positions that served British interests. Our own scholars and politicians played their part in arriving at twisted historical conclusions. And here, the major responsibility must lie with anti-Hindus.

Maulana Muhammad Ali, who was the principal lieutenant of Mahatma Gandhi during his *satyagraha* campaign of 1920-21, refused to join him in the second campaign in 1930. At a meeting of the All India Muslim Conference in Bombay in April 1930, attended by over 20,000 Muslims, he bluntly stated: 'We refuse to join Mr Gandhi because his movement is not a movement for the complete independence of India but for making the seventy millions of Indian Musalmans dependents of the Hindu Mahasabha'.

The Maulana made no secret of the fact that the Muslims, as a whole, were guided by pan-Islamism. He told members of the Round Table Conference in London that Islam was not confined to India. 'I belong', said he, 'to two circles of equal size

---

20 Jaziya is a per capita yearly tax historically levied by Islamic states on certain non-Muslim subjects—dhimmis—permanently residing in Muslim lands under Islamic law.

but which are not concentric. One is India and the other is the Muslim world. We are not nationalists but supra-nationalists'. In his address as Congress President in 1923, Maulana Muhammad Ali reminded the audience that extraterritorial sympathies were a part of the quintessence of Islam, as stated by RC Majumdar in *History of the Freedom Movement in India*, Volume III, Firma KL Mukhopadhyay, Calcutta 1977.

As is well known, Muhammad Ali and his brother Shaukat Ali were followers of Mahatma Gandhi when he led the Khilafat movement to protect the throne of the Sultan of Turkey and the caliphate of all Sunni Muslims in the world. They lost all interest in Gandhi when, in 1924, Kemal Ataturk, the Turkish general, exiled the sultan and abolished the Caliphate.

Now read a few highlights from the *Lal Ishtihar* or the Red Pamphlet written by one Ibrahim Khan of Mymensingh district in East Bengal early in the 20th century; refer to page 108 of *Struggle for Freedom* by R C Majumdar, Bharatiya Vidya Bhawan, Bombay, 1988.

> Ye Musalmans! Arise, awake! Do not read in the same schools with Hindus. Do not buy anything from a Hindu shop. Do not touch any article manufactured by Hindu hands. Do not give any employment to a Hindu. Do not accept any degrading office under a Hindu. You are ignorant. But if you acquire knowledge you can at once send all Hindus to *jahannum* (hell). You form the majority of the population of this province.
>
> Among the cultivators also you form the majority. It is agriculture that is the source of wealth. The Hindu has no wealth of his own and has made himself rich only by despoiling you of your wealth. If you become sufficiently enlightened, then the Hindus will starve and soon become Mohammedans.
>
> Hindus are very selfish. As the progress of Mohammedans is inimical to the self-aggrandisement of Hindus, the latter

> will always oppose Mohammedan progress for their selfish ends. Be united in boycotting Hindus. What dire mischief have they not done to us! They have robbed us of honour and wealth. They have deprived us of our daily bread. And now they are going to deprive us of our very life.

Evidently, these are not the ravings of a normal person. Yet the depth of emotion is reflective of the deep divide between the two communities. British manipulation to divide Indians could not be compared to such venom, nor could any administration responsible for law and order possibly encourage such emotions. This does not mean that the British did not take tactical advantage of the differences, in order to sustain their rule. The point that is being made is that the divide was old and deep and the British were only the beneficiaries.

Decades have passed since the British left the sub-continent. Yet the tension between the two communities continues, between India and Pakistan, between India and Bangladesh and between the Hindus and Muslims. Why? Because, as Professor S Abid Husain, former Secretary, Government of India, has lucidly explained in *The National Culture of India* (National Book Trust, 1972):

> Like other Indian communities and most Asian peoples, while honour is as sacred as the values of patriotism and loyalty to the state, Muslims are unanimous in rejecting what Western nations explicitly believe in, the priority of country or state over religion.

The Hindu confirmation of these Muslim contentions is given by Nirad C Chaudhuri in his *Autobiography of an Unknown Indian*, Macmillan & Company Limited, London, 1951.

> When I see the gigantic catastrophe of Hindu-Muslim discord of these days I am not surprised because we as

children held the tiny mustard seed in our hands and sowed it very diligently. In fact, this conflict was implicit in the very unfolding of our history and could hardly be avoided. Heaven preserve me from dishonesty, so general among Indians, of attributing this conflict to British rule, however much the foreign rulers might have profited by it. Indeed they would have been excusable only as gods and not as man the political animal, had they made no use of the weapon so assiduously manufactured by us and by us also put into their hands. But even then, they did not make use of it to the extent they might easily have done. This I know is a very controversial thesis but I think it can be easily proved if we do not turn a blind eye to the facts of our history.

A British view of the schism between the two communities is provided by Sir Percival Griffiths, ICS, in his book *The British Impact on India* (Macdonald & Company Limited, London; 1952).

India stood sharply divided between Hindus and Muslims. The feelings between them were much what could be expected since one community had been dominant and the other subject and often though not always oppressed. What is today called communal dissension was thus the permanent and inevitable legacy of centuries of Muslim rule.

Much has been made of the separate electorates as an attempt by the British to divide and rule. Here is what Sir Percival had to say:

Indian politicians have bitterly reproached Britain for introducing the principle of communal electorates in the Morley-Minto reforms. In reality, there was no practical alternative. If semi-parliamentary bodies such as the Morley-Minto Councils were to mean anything at all, it was essential that all communities should be genuinely represented in them. *The gulf between the Hindus and the Muslims at that time was wide and nobody with experience of modern India will doubt that under any system of joint electorates the Hindus would have secured the return of non-representative Muslims.* The philosopher might deplore the fact that Hindus and Muslims thought of themselves as separate peoples but the statesman had to accept it. The fears of the Muslims were real and deep-seated. When the Congress leaders some years later formed a temporary alliance with the Muslims they too had to recognise those fears; perhaps the greatest justification of the British establishment of communal electorates lies in the fact that they were recognised in 1916 by the Lucknow Pact between the Congress Party and the Muslim League.

The Taliban—the Offspring of the Deobandi Movement

The Taliban presents the most glaring example of Dar-ul-Islam in today's times.

In 1996, after seizing power in Afghanistan, when the Taliban ordered the Hindus there to wear yellow in order not be mistaken as Muslims many, including American Senators, were outraged. There was similar outrage earlier during the Bamiyan episode, when very ancient statues of the Buddha were destroyed. The Taliban barbarism can be understood only when one understands some of the fundamentals of Islam.

To be made to wear yellow meant being declared as a protected citizen or a dhimmi, which means someone who was not a momin but a non-believer who had paid his taxes or jaziya. This tradition of levying poll tax originated in the Holy Quran. A non-Muslim subject of a Muslim state belonging to the Jewish, Christian, or Sabean creed by the payment of a poll tax, enjoyed security of person and property in a Mohammedan country. To adhere to this tradition was to be faithful to the Book. In Judaic ethos, humanity has invariably been classified into two sections; the faithful and non-believers. There were the Jews and the gentiles, the Christians and the heathens, the momins and the kafirs. The Taliban was being forthright. Christians are theologically discriminatory about the heathens, although in practice they are less candid about their beliefs. Nevertheless, evangelists continue to proselytise in many parts of the world.

His Holiness, the Pope, as recently as 2000 AD, declared that there was a harvest of souls to be reaped in Asia. It also needs to be remembered that Christian theology did not provide any formal option to the nonbelievers. Communists were openly totalitarian and gave no space to anyone who happened to differ. Anyone who was even remotely bourgeois was either exiled or liquidated. Whereas the Muslims did allow an alternative by offering to confer a dhimmi status for those prepared to pay jaziya. The status carried preconditions such as wearing yellow for the Jews and blue for the Christians. Hindus and others came to be offered this status after the conquest of Hindustan. The Pact of Umar II signed with the Jews and Christians is relevant. Umar II ruled as Khalifa at Mecca between 632 AD and 634 AD. In his endeavour to preserve the integrity of the Caliphate, he opened many dialogues with other communities. The pact being quoted is the result of such a dialogue. What non-Muslim communities conceded to Umar is quoted:

- We shall not build in our cities or in their vicinity any new monasteries, churches, hermitages, or monks cells. We shall not restore, by night or by day, any of them that have fallen into ruin or which are located in the Muslims' quarters.
- We shall keep our gates wide open for the passerby and travellers. We shall provide three days food and lodging to any Muslims who pass our way.
- We shall not shelter any spy in our churches or in our homes, nor shall we hide him from the Muslims.

- We shall not teach our children the Quran.
- We shall not hold public religious ceremonies. We shall not seek to proselytize anyone. We shall not prevent any of our kin from embracing Islam if they so desire.
- We shall show deference to the Muslims and shall rise from our seats when they wish to sit down.
- We shall not attempt to resemble the Muslims in any way.
- We shall not ride on saddle.
- We shall not wear swords or bear weapons of any kind, or even carry them with us.
- We shall not sell wines.
- We shall clip the forelocks of our head.
- We shall not display our books anywhere in the Muslim thoroughfares or in their marketplaces. We shall only beat our clappers in our churches very quietly. We shall not raise our voices when reciting the service in our churches, nor when in the presence of Muslims. Neither shall we raise our voices in our funeral processions.
- We shall not build our homes higher than theirs.

In fact, the Taliban are absolute fundamentalists. A fundamentalist is one who follows and quotes the scriptures in any argument. The Taliban in the 21st century epitomises an example par excellence of fundamentalism.

The Bamiyan episode (2001) and the iconoclasm it personifies made Hindus virtually weep. Hindus feel the same way when they visit the Udaygiri caves near Vidisha in Madhya Pradesh. But to someone wedded to another ideology, such destruction must have appeared pious. The cornerstone of the Judaic ethos has been monotheism or an absolute faith in one god. In the eyes of a Jew, a Christian or a Muslim, even a suggestion, or a hint of an alternative deity to his God is abomination, which explains the objection to the sight of an idol or an image for possible worship. Prophet Mohammad was so scrupulous that he did not distinguish between an idol for worship and an ordinary statue. He did not want to take any chance by allowing any discretion of choice to his followers. He, therefore, did not permit the use of imagery whether of animal, man or god. Portraits, statues, paintings etc. were forbidden, lest they attracted devotion in competition to Allah. This commandment applied not only for the future but the Prophet also saw danger even in the past, in all idols and statues that existed.

As the *First Encyclopaedia of Islam* puts it, all the accumulation of heathendom, which had gathered round the Kaba, was now thrust aside. As many as 360 idols are said to have stood around the building. 'When touched with the Prophet's rod, they all fell to the ground.' The statue of Hubal, which Amr B Luhaiy is said to have erected over the pit inside the Kaba, was removed as well as the representations of the prophets. In the light of this command, what the Taliban did at Bamiyan was in consonance with the fundamentals of their faith. The Taliban even today imposes principles of conduct that were relevant to Muslims 1,400 years ago in Arabia, and should have changed since. But they insist on being consistent with the pristine fundamentals of Islam.

Not many know it, but the fact is that the ideology and thinking that has given birth to Islamic fundamentalist—and terrorist—organisations like the Taliban has its roots in an obscurantist movement that has its origins in a little known town in India.

The town is Deoband, a mere 150 km away from India's capital Delhi. And the system of education that spawns outfits like the Taliban originates in Muslim seminaries, called *maktaba*s or *madrasa*s.

The traditional Muslim system of education in India is the same as found elsewhere in the Muslim world. There is the maktaba (mosque school), where elementary principles of reading and writing are taught, as well as the reading of the Quran, and elements of religious law (*fiqh*). Beyond the maktaba is the madrasa (college), commonly called also Dar-ul-Uloom (abode of the sciences). The first record we have of a madrasa being founded in India dates from the year 1191 AD when Muhammad Ghori during his conquest of Ajmer, is said to have destroyed pillars and foundation of the idol temples, and built in their stead mosques and colleges. Other rulers who followed did the same.

In present times, the most important of all the Indian madrasas is also at this small city of Deoband in the Saharanpur district of western Uttar Pradesh. The Dar-ul-Uloom there is to India what the university at al-Azhar, in Cairo, is to Egypt and the Near East. From these madrasas, found all over the land, teachers now, as formerly, go out to teach in the maktabas or mosque schools, even to the remotest towns and villages (pp 76-77, *Indian Islam* by Murray T Titus, Oxford University Press, 1937).

The Al-Wahhabi Movement

In the 18th century, there emerged in Arabia a movement dedicated to the destruction of all interpretations of religion other than its own.[21] Charles Allen, a renowned historian of the British Raj, in his book, *God's Terrorists* (Brown Book Group, London) states that during his great grandfather's time this was known as Al-Wahhabi—the Wahhabi. The Viceroy of India, Lord Mayo was knifed by a Wahhabi-directed assassin in 1871 in Andaman Islands. The British authorities in India

21 Wahhabism is named after an eighteenth-century preacher and activist, Muhammad ibn Abd al-Wahhab (1703–1792). He started a reform movement in the remote, sparsely populated region of Najd in Saudi Arabia. advocating a purging of such widespread Sunni practices as the veneration of saints and the visiting of their tombs and shrines.

termed these *Wahhabis* as the 'Hindustani Fanatics' with their base in the mountains of the North-Western Frontier (now in Pakistan). In his grandparents' time, the movement reappeared on the Arabian peninsula and called itself as *Al-Ikhwan*. In our days, from these movements two different branches appeared—one tight-knit and locally called the Taliban and the other loose-knit with global aspirations called *al-Qaeda*.

Jamaat Ahl-i-Hadith

After the failure of 1857 mutiny, and the deportation of the Mughal Emperor to Rangoon in 1858, the British rulers set up Edwardes College in Peshawar and Aitchison College in Lahore where the sons of former governing aristocracy could be educated on English lines.

The Muslim community got divided in two groups on the question of modern learning. One group headed by Syed Ahmad Khan favoured western education. The other group who favoured a backward leap was headed by Shah Muhammad Ishaq and Sayyid Nazir Husain who were educated in the tradition of Shah Waliullah,[22] an Islamic reformer, in the years before the Mutiny of 1857. Sayyid Nazir Hussain had led the Wahhabi Delhi-ites in 1857. These were the alumni of the Jamaat Madrassah-i-Rahimiya in Delhi. They were arrested by the British. After their release, they formed a politico-religious organisation known as *Jamaat Ahl-i-Hadith*, the Party of the People of the Hadith. Their openly declared aim was to convert India into an abode of Islam through jihad. Even today, its unremitting anti-polytheist, anti-innovation, anti-Shia and anti-Christian message continues to attract a hard core of fundamentalist Sunnis, says Charles Allen.

22 Shah Waliullah Dehlawi (1703–1762). His father, Shah Abdur Rahim was the founder of the Madrasah-i Rahimiyah.

The Madrasa at Deoband

In May 1866, Muhammad Qasim and Rashid Ahmed, two of the four-man group of jihadis that had left Delhi in 1857 established their madrasa at Deoband, seventy-five miles north of Delhi. Initially the school was known as Arab Madrasa and it had one teacher, Mullah Mahmood Deobandi, and one student Mahmood ul-Hassan. Muhammad Qasim wrote: 'The English have perpetrated boundless acts of tyranny against the Muslims for their fault, if at all it was a fault, of the uprising of 1857 and their relentless endeavours for the independence of the country thereafter. They have left no stone unturned to plunder and obliterate the Islamic arts and science, Muslim culture and civilisation.'

Teaching of English was prohibited at the school. All classes were focused on Quranic studies and great emphasis was laid on the doctrine of oneness as taught by Shah Waliullah and his descendants Shah Abdul Aziz and Shah Muhammad Ishaq. Deoband denounced the worship of saints, the adorning of tombs, and such activities as music and dancing; it waged a ceaseless war of words against Shias, Hindus and Christian missionaries. It retained militant jihad as a central pillar of faith, but focused this jihad on the promotion of Islamic revival and identity through the principles of the immutability of Sharia, the oneness of God and the overreaching, guiding authority of the Ulema.

Fatwa by Dar-ul-Ulum Deoband

In turn, the institution came to be seen in India as the last word on all matters pertaining to Sharia and how a good Muslim should behave. One of the earliest fatwas given by the Madrasa declared the activities of Syed Ahmad Khan as un-Islamic. Deoband became known throughout India as the place where boys could be safely initiated into the old religion of their forefathers. In 1879, the institution assumed the additional name of Dar-ul-Uloom, the abode of Islamic learning.

The Salafis

By the end of the 19th century Dar-ul-Uloom Deoband had founded more than two dozen madrasas in northern India. At about the same time, these teachings of the institution were dignified with the term *salafi* or following the forefathers, first developed by the medieval *Hanbali* jurist of Damascus, Ibn Taymiyya. Those who followed forefathers' teachings became known as *salafiyya.*

The impact of Dar-ul-Uloom was immense and worldwide. Its teachings gave new impetus to the old ideas: that a true Muslim's first duty was to his religion; that his only country was the world community of Islam; and that he had an obligation to defend wherever it was under attack. The end result was a seismic shift in the Sunni Islam of South Asia, which became increasingly conservative and introvert, less tolerant, and far more inclined to look for political leadership to the madrasa and the madrasa-trained political leaders committed to the cause of leading the ummah back to the true faith. The consequences were profound (pages 210-211 of Allen's book).

In September, 1878 Lord Lytton sent a mission to Kabul to tell the Amir of Kabul that he should avoid having any political connection with Russia. The Amir snubbed the mission and warned it not to enter Afghan territory. Thus began the Second Afghan War. Though British won the war, the real victor was Abdur Rahman, the Amir of Kabul who declared himself as a *Mujtahid* and crushed all rebellion, vanquished the Shias and incorporated Kafirstan into Afghanistan, renaming it Nooristan.

When an Ulema accused the Amir of infidelity, he killed him with his own hands. But he was unhappy with the British as they had taken away large chunks of land from Afghanistan by drawing the Durand Line in November 1893. In response to British forward policy, Abdur Rahman tried to consolidate the Pathans and declared himself as *Zia-ul-Millat wa-ud-Deen* (Light of Union and Faith).

Rise of Jamal al-Din Afghani

Muslim intellectuals took advantage of this policy. Sayyid Jamal al-Din Afghani was among the first to declare that Britain was Islam's greatest enemy. Expelled by Abdur Rahman, he reappeared in India and opposed Syed Ahmad Khan's policies. He advocated pan-Islamism and this inspired radicals throughout the Muslim world. The result was the formation of two anti-imperialist political movements: the *Ikhwan-ul-Muslimeen*, the Muslim Brotherhood in Egypt and *Jamaat-i-Islami*, the Party of Islam in India.

Observation by Frank Martin

This is what Frank Martin, who worked as Chief Engineer to Abdur Rahman, wrote in 1895: 'The sight of a *kafar*, and all who are not Mussulman or infidels, is so obnoxious that they spit in the street, and to kill one of them is quite a meritorious action in their eye... They argue that the enemy of their religion is the enemy of God... and the Quran commands them to kill all such, and promises that if they themselves are killed in doing so, they shall go straight to Paradise...' (page 216 of Allen's book).

Another Englishman, Lionel James of Reuters, writing three years later in 1898 observed: 'One is inclined to sum up the cause of the outbreak under three heads, the first of which is fanaticism, the second fanaticism, and the third fanaticism.'

Teachings of Syed Ahmad Barelvi

In the mid 1890 the situation was very tense on the Afghan frontier as Pathan tribes were intent upon waging a jihad against the British. The Ottoman Sultan had recently won victories against Christians in Greece, Turks had captured Suez Canal and Aden. The inspiration for all this rebellious movement was provided by Syed Ahmad, the first Hindustani fanatic. He was born in 1786 in Rae Bareili. A student of Abd al-Aziz,

Syed Ahmad Barelvi (1786-1831) developed the theme of jihad more fully and ultimately led a holy war to establish a new, strictly Islamic state and society in India. He began work to establish his new Islamic state in the North West Frontier Areas and assumed the title of Imam and commander of the faithful.

Conference at Dar-ul-Uloom

In April 1911, a conference of Dar-ul-Uloom, Deoband Madrasa was held, presided over by Mahmood ul-Hasan. He was the first student of the institution in 1866. In collaboration with Deoband's co-founder Muhammad Qasim, he had set up an organisation called *Samaratut Tarbiyat* (Results of the Training). This was a quasi-military body in which volunteers known as *fidayeen*, or men of sacrifice, were taught to prepare themselves for armed jihad against the British. With the death of Muhammad Qasim in 1880, the leadership of the Deoband passed on to the co-founder Rashid Ahmad and after his death in 1905, to Mahmood ul-Hasan.

As a rector of Dar-ul-Uloom, Mahmood Hasan continued to propagate the strict pro-*tawhid* (staunch monotheism), pro-ulema, anti-innovation, anti-polytheism, fundamentalist revivalism first initiated in Syria by Ibn Taymiyya, in Arabia by Al-Wahhab, and in India by Shah Waliullah. While addressing the delegates Hasan declared that the time had come to resume the armed struggle against the British colonial government in India. Did Maulana Muhammad Qasim found this madrasa only for teaching and learning? Far from it. It was founded in 1866 to teach and prepare Muslims to make up for the losses of 1857 (page 262 of Allen's book). The quasi-military organisation was reconstituted as *Jamiat-ul-Ansaar*, the Party of Volunteers.

Hijrat

In 1914, Qasim put into execution his plan for hijra similar to that drawn up by Syed Ahmad Barelvi a century earlier. His followers at once took up the call of the Sultan of Turkey for Muslims to unite in jihad against Britain. Despite claims to the contrary that Dar-ul-Uloom was not engaged in jihad, Charles Allen concludes: 'But enough details survive to give the lie to those who claim that the Dar ul-Uloom Deoband was never in the business of promoting jihad' (page 265 of the book).

The Silk Letter Conspiracy

In 1915, no fewer than 222 clerics gathered from all over northern India in what came to be known later as the Silk Letter Conspiracy Case.[23] A large proportion of these arrestees were Deobandi alumni. The traitorous actions of Mahmood ul-Hasan and his associates were publicly repudiated by the Dar ul-Uloom Deoband authorities, who were unable to show the British Governor in India that they had severed all links with his organisation long before war. In 1920, Deoband formed the Jamiat-i-Ulema-i-Hind (JUH). In the hijrat movement launched by Sunni Muslims during the First World War, Sayyid Abul A'la Maududi took a leading part. He was associated with Deobandi JUH led by Maulana Hussain Ahmad Madani. JUH's alliance with the Congress led to two splinter groups: one led by Maulana Muhammad Ilyar whose party *Tablighi Jamiat* (Preaching Party) followed the teachings of Shah Waliullah and the other led by Mawdoodi set up the Jamiat-i-Islami in Lahore. As demands grew for a separate Muslim nation-state, Deobandis formed the Jamiat-i-Ulema-i-Islam in 1945 whose declared aim was to shape the new nation of Pakistan into a truly Muslim state.

---

23 The Silk Letter Conspiracy refers to a movement organised by the Deobandi leaders between 1913 and 1920, aimed at freeing India from the British rule by allying with Ottoman Turkey, Imperial Germany, and Afghanistan. The plot was uncovered by Punjab CID with the capture of letters from Ubaidullah Sindhi, one of the Deobandi leaders then in Afghanistan, to Mahmood ul-Hasan, another leader then in Persia. The letters were written on silk cloth, hence the name.

Influence of Deobandis in Pakistan

In 1972, in Pakistan 40 per cent of the madrasas were Deobandi; by the end of 1980, this rose to 65 per cent. In 2002, out of the total 10,000 madrasas 7,000 were Deobandis. For the jihad against Soviet Afghanistan in the 1980s, an increasing number of madrasas had become indoctrination and training schools.

In early April, 2001 a vast encampment of canvas tents and brightly coloured cotton shamianas sprang up on the plains beside the village of Taro Jaba on the eastern limits of the Vale of Peshawar (the trans-Indus plain). Over the course of three days what was reported as the largest gathering ever seen in Pakistan celebrated the achievements of the Dar-ul-Uloom Deoband Madrasa Movement. Two speeches received the greatest acclaim—one from Mullah Omar and the other from Osama bin Laden. Maulana Fazal-ur-Rahman presided over the conference. Mullah Omar would later go on to be the foremost figure of the Taliban and a globally wanted terrorist.

Rise of Fanaticism in Afghanistan

'There is no God but Allah, and Mohammed is the prophet of Allah.' Such is the cry that electrifies nearly a billion inhabitants of this globe. Such is the cry which so thrills millions among them that they are ready to go forward and fight for their religion, and consider it a short road to paradise to kill Christians, Hindus and unbelievers.

'It is that cry which at the present time is echoing and re-echoing through the hills and mountain fastnesses of the North-West Frontier of India. It is that cry the mullahs of Afghanistan are now carrying to mountain hamlets and to towns in Afghanistan in order to raise the people of that country to come forward and fight. That is a cry which has the power of joining together the members of Islam throughout the world, and preparing them for a conflict with all who are not ready to accept their religion. And it is especially these Mohammedans on the North-West Frontier of India who have this intense religious zeal—call it what we will, fanaticism or bigotry—but which, nevertheless, is a power within them overruling every passion' (Dr Theodore Pennell, Missionary Doctor at Bannu, *Among the Wild Tribes of the Afghan Frontier,* 1909).

The Taliban

Initially hailed as liberators who secured towns, made the streets safe and cleaned up corruption and graft, the Taliban's strict forms of Islam soon became a terror. Their doctrines mirror those of Saudi Arabia's Wahhabi religious establishment and Pakistan's Jamaat-i-Islami. They segregated the sexes outside the home, closed girls' schools, required that women be fully covered in public and banned women from the workplace. They also banned television, cinema and music, ordered men to grow beards and pray five times a day and introduced the *hudud* punishments as prescribed by the Quran and Hadith, such as amputation for theft, death for murder, stoning for adultery (*The Oxford History of Islam*; OUP, New York, 1999).

Islamic Law

When speaking about Islamic law, informed Muslims use the term Shariah to connote the sacred law as a global concept, while the fiqh is used to connote the ongoing interpretation of the law through the four Sunni school of jurisdical practice. The Shariah developed as the model of the Islamic way of life, whereas the fiqh, the application of the Shariat[24] to specific cases. A common belief fostered by modem political Islamists is that only the Shariah constitutes the true law of God and not the fiqh. This negative view of Islamic jurisprudence—which is advocated by such groups as the Muslim Brotherhood

24 Provisions of the Quran.

of Egypt, the Jamaat-i-Islami of Pakistan and the Taliban of Afghanistan—ignores the essential complementarity of Shariat and fiqh and threatens to deny Islamic law the ability to adapt to changing conditions (*The Oxford History of Islam).*

Hindus Betrayed by their Politicians

The Muslim League demanded an exchange of population especially through 1946. Simultaneously, it carried on Direct Action, following the Great Calcutta Killings of August 1946, especially in the Punjab, where the party felt ethnic cleansing was most necessary. Come 1947, the rioting escalated in order to make sure that the Hindus, including Sikhs, emigrated. The carnage continued after Independence; by 1948, the western wing of Pakistan had been cleansed of Hindus and Sikhs. The eastern wing, or what is now Bangladesh, was emulating the western wing, although at a more gradual pace.

In sharp contrast, Congress leaders, whether in government or outside, ignored the League's demand for an exchange of population. Mahatma Gandhi kept up the chant *Ishwar Allah Tero Nam* throughout his life, repeating that Ram and Rahim were one. Although Jawaharlal Nehru called himself a British prime minister of India, he behaved like a Muslim although he happened to be a Hindu. He had come to be known as a Fabian or non-revolutionary socialist. A socialist had to be spontaneously secular. At the same time Nehru took pride in being known as 'a British prime minister' of India. Vallabhbhai Patel was about the only top Congressman who warned Muslims that those who did not emigrate to Pakistan had to be loyal to *Hindustan.*

How far Nehru was impartial between religions and whether he was biased is best verified by what is codified in the Constitution of India whose passing he led and directed as Prime Minister.

Article 29: Protection of Interests of Minorities

- Any section of the citizens residing in the territory of India or any part thereof having a distinct language, script or culture of its own shall have the right to conserve the same.
- No citizen shall be denied admission into any educational institution maintained by the state or receiving aid out of state funds on grounds only of religion, race, caste, language or any of them.

Article 30: Right of Minorities to Establish and Administer Educational Institutions

All minorities, whether based on religion or language, shall have the right to establish and administer educational institutions of their choice.

1(A) In making any law providing for the compulsory acquisition of any property of an educational institution established and administered by a minority, referred to in clause (1), the state shall ensure that the amount fixed by or determined under such law for the acquisition of such property is such as would not restrict or abrogate the right guaranteed under that clause.

The state shall not, in granting aid to educational institutions, discriminate against any educational institution on the ground that it is under the management of a minority, whether based on religion or language.

These articles were based on what was drafted well before Partition had been decided. Speaking in the Constituent Assembly on 8th December 1948, Jawaharlal Nehru said:

> Mr Vice President. Sir, we are on the last lap of our long journey. Nearly two years ago, we met in this hall and on that solemn occasion it was my high privilege to move a resolution which has come to be known as the Objective Resolution. This is rather a prosaic description of that

> resolution because it embodied something more than mere objectives although objectives are big things in the life of a nation. It tried to embody in so far as it is possible in cold print the spirit that lay behind the Indian people at the time. It is difficult to maintain the spirit of a nation or a people at a high level all the time and I do not know if we have succeeded in doing that. Nevertheless, I hope that it is in that spirit that we shall consider it in detail always using that Objective Resolution as the yard measure with which to test every clause and phrase in this Constitution.

The Objective Resolution was introduced in the same Constituent Assembly by Jawaharlal Nehru on 13th December 1946 well before the decision had been taken by the British government, the Communist Party, the Muslim League and others to partition the country.

Even the declaration by the British Prime Minister, Clement Attlee, that India would be granted independence was not made until 20th February 1947. The final decision to partition the country had to wait till 3rd June 1947.

There were eight clauses in the Objective Resolution of which No.6 read: 'Wherein adequate safeguards shall be provided for minorities, backward and tribal areas, and depressed and other backward, evidently the privileges contemplated for the minorities were an endeavour to avoid Partition by dissuading the Muslims, especially the League, from insisting on division of the country. Nevertheless, the League successfully insisted on the implementation of the two-nation theory, whereby it was Pakistan for the Muslims and Hindustan for the rest. Even though it may be difficult to accept that in this context even for the Muslims, Jinnah was more reasonable than Nehru. The proof of this contention is the agreement that Jinnah signed with Raja Maheshwar Dayal Seth, General Secretary of the All India Hindu Mahasabha, several years before Partition. The essence of the agreement was that in the event of Partition, Muslims would not expect any safeguards in Hindustan.

What is Secular?

Although secularism to this day remains the signature tune of the Congress party, yet faith in its ideals has never taken root. In fact, what precisely secularism means in India has never been clarified. The 16th century European definition was separation of the church from the state; non-interference of the clergy in affairs of government. The Marxist concept was to abolish all religion from the life of the people, whereas tolerance has been a hallmark of the Hindu ethos since the beginning. Therefore, the question of introducing 'secularism' into the affairs of India is unnecessary. The way secularism has been practiced in India has distorted the spirit of tolerance. Hindu-Muslim riots are a symptom of this distortion.

It is noteworthy that of the constitutions of 39 countries that I have seen, only four mention the word *secular*. They are the Albanian, French, Indian and Namibian constitutions. Incidentally, when our Constitution was adopted in 1950, there was no mention of secularism. The term was brought in by Indira Gandhi during the Emergency in 1976. Many an opposition member was then in jail. Nevertheless, had the Indian state remained impartial towards all religions, the distortion of tolerance might not have been so widespread. Unfortunately, government policies have shown a distinct bias towards the Muslims. For example, the Haj subsidy; no comparable concession is provided to members of any other faith. If a Roman Catholic proposes to go to the Vatican, he has to pay the full fare for his trip. So has a Jew if he were to go to Jerusalem. The Hindu does not get anything for going on a pilgrimage.

One of the directive principles of policy contained in Article 44 of the Constitution requires the introduction of a common civil code; one law common to all citizens. Sixty-seven years have passed since the Constitution was adopted, yet there is no sign of the country having a single civil code. If the Muslims were to insist on their own distinctive personal law, why should the state not also demand of them to accept the Sharia with regard to criminal law? Minority educational institutions are allowed to be run freely although they are subsidised by the state, whereas, Hindu institutions are denied any subsidy. So discriminatory is this law that the much-respected Ramakrishna Mission was driven to claim that it is a minority organisation!

Why was the Minorities Commission established? Are not minorities human? Their interests could have been looked after by the National Human Rights Commission. Evidently, there was systematic intention on the part of the Government of India at some point in time to keep alight the flame of minorityism. If they get integrated into the national mainstream, they might cease to be useful vote banks!

It is unlikely that the Muslim community or its leadership initially demanded any of these favours from the Indian state. Who would understand Muslim aspirations better than Qaid-e-Azam Jinnah, especially in the years around Independence and partition? It is not widely known that Jinnah entered into a written agreement, several years before partition, with the All India Hindu Mahasabha, whose General Secretary at the time was Raja Maheshwar Dayal Seth According to the agreement, the country was to be partitioned soon after Independence with the help of a plebiscite. There was to be no corridor between the Muslim areas of the northwest and the northeast of India although they could form a single sovereign state. Government machinery was to be provided for facilitating the transfer of population. Above all, it said: 'In the event of separation the Muslims shall not demand any safeguard for the Muslim minority in Hindustan. It will be open to the two Indias to arrange on a reciprocal basis safeguards for religious minorities in the respective states' (Page 301, *Indian Muslim*: A *Political History* by Ram Gopal, Asia Publishing House, New York, 1959).

How the minorities were dealt with subsequently by Pakistan is well known. Rafiq Zakaria, in his recent book *The Man Who Divided India*; Popular Prakashan, Mumbai, 2001, has described what happened in that country. Some Indian Muslims living in India asked Mr Jinnah on the eve of partition:

> 'What is to happen to us who are being left behind?' He assured them that if any harm came to them, Pakistan would retaliate against the Hindus under its control. But he could not have been serious about that for he must have known that after the hate campaign he had unleashed against the Hindus, few of them would have dared to stay on in his Pakistan and they did not; they fled in the most excruciating circumstances—many died on the way, the rest reached India with nothing.

Although the expression 'ethnic cleansing' was not used, what happened in the western wing of Pakistan was just that. The same has been happening in the eastern wing, but in a chronic, rather than acute manner.

In fairness to the Muslim League and the community it represented, it was forthright about its non-secular intentions ever since it was founded in 1906. One of its essential rules was that only a Muslim could become a member of the party. The League's demand for separate electorates was conceded by the Lucknow Pact, which was signed between the Congress and the Muslim League in 1916. While writing in his journal *Al Hilal* during 1913, Maulana Abul Kalam Azad had said that no Muslim need join any political party. Islam itself is a party whose name is Hizbullah. The Imam and the Sultan are rolled into one and this integrated concept was personified by the Caliph or the representative of the Holy Prophet.

The Congress, by conceding separate electorates for the two communities, only buried its secular credentials.

Whatever hope might have persisted for the practice of secularism in India, was finally dashed when the Congress conceded the League's demand for Partition. Pakistan for Muslims and Hindustan for the rest was the understanding of the League.

No matter what the ideals of the Congress leaders might have been, to agree to Partition was to endorse the two-nation Theory. The Muslims of undivided India, it was contended by the League, were a nation separate from the rest of Indians. They, therefore, needed a separate homeland. Pakistan was not merely a piece of territory vivisected from the rest of India. It was also a home for all the Muslims to gather in, to live in and flourish. The Congress let the country's territory be divided, but did not follow through with the transfer of people. Instead, its government enshrined discriminatory temptations—Articles 29 and 30, in the Constitution to induce Muslims to stay back.

The failure of Hindustan to fall in line with Islamic separatism was unfortunate, if not also unwarranted.

New Delhi appointed as its first High Commissioner to Pakistan a gentleman called Sri Prakasa who proved to be a quisling or *gaddar*. Read in his own words as printed in his book called *Pakistan: Birth and Early Days,* published by Meenakshi Prakashan, Delhi, 1965.

> Our Government did its very best to make it possible for Muslims to come back to India. Naturally, they could not take everyone. The problem of sheer accommodation was exceedingly difficult. We had to find room for many millions of Punjabi and Sindhi Hindus; and we could not possibly have all the Muslims also with us even though we had no animosity for them and we really desired that they should stay with us.

I had to face three exoduses. I have already spoken of the employees of the Central Government and then of Sindhi Hindus. The third was of Indian Muslims who had come to Pakistan in a fit of great enthusiasm for a new homeland that they had obtained and where they have hoped that prosperity would be waiting with open arms to welcome them.

To the Banaras weavers, I said: 'Why have you come here? No one wants you here. Do get back home. Why do you want to destroy my city? It is you who have made it famous in the world'. I immediately used to issue permits to them to go back. This caused some misunderstanding between me and my assistants in my office. They looked at the situation with different eyes. The Government of India also later changed its policy in this behalf (*sic.*). Formerly, they encouraged Indian Muslims to remain where they were. Later, when they saw that not a single Hindu was allowed to remain in Pakistan and that all of them were coming away, they felt it was necessary that at least as many Muslims should go away as was the number of Hindus who had come. There was obviously not sufficient room for everyone in India as she now became.

Constitutionally speaking, I was more responsible for them because they were Indians than for the Hindus in Pakistan because these were the primary charge of the government there. The situation being what it was at that time, the position was reversed; and the Indian High Commission came to be in a way in charge of the welfare of the Hindus in Pakistan while the Government of Pakistan was supposed to have the duty of looking after migrating Indian Muslims.

Muslim Backwardness, AMU and Separatism

Legacy of Syed Ahmad and Nehru

Sir Syed Ahmad Khan was the first Muslim leader of modern India. By being one of the few UP Muslims to have been on the side of the British during the Mutiny of 1857, he wielded considerable influence with the rulers. He was a member of the Viceroy's Executive Council. He was also the first to declare in 1887 that the Hindus and Muslims were separate nations. His co-religionists, being smaller in number, had to have reservation in government services as well as in electoral bodies that may come up. His example was an encouragement to the community to practise the Islamic ethos which in essence is non-commercial and not greatly concerned about its production. It prefers to live off nature's bounty, including the womenfolk.

The ethos does not lay much store by way of saving or capital accumulation. Muslims rely on Allah to look after them in their hour of need if and when need be. As it happened, nature's bounty was generously bestowed upon the Indo Gangetic plain as well as the land of the Brahmaputra. UP, Bihar, Bengal or

Assam which is where there are more Muslims than in other parts of divided India. And little wonder that the easy going economic habit infected the non-Muslims in this whole belt that is described as backward and, by and large, poorer. Bengal, which was flourishing with industry at Independence, gradually became the graveyard of factories. The fate of Kanpur was also the fate of the whole belt that stretches from Saharanpur in the west to Kamrup in the east.

Partition was meant to bring to a close the mischief of Sir Syed and his two-nation theory. MA Jinnah and at least seven of his League colleagues had demanded an exchange of populations whereby most Muslims would settle in Pakistan and most non-Muslims would live in Hindustan. Led by Jawaharlal Nehru, the Congress and its government obstructed this final solution and instead resumed accommodating the two nations all over again in the Hindustan post 1947. In order to counter the Patelites or the nationalists in the Congress, Nehru played to the Muslim gallery and pampered its members more than he would his own children. If any Hindu leader was loved by Muslims, it was Nehru. Sardar Patel described him as the only nationalist Muslim there was.

Nehru ruled India as an unquestioned *badshah* for 17 long years and, as it were, pushed this backward belt from Saharanpur to Kamrup deeper into a non-productive culture. It continues to be the most backward and, by and large, the poorest in the country. No one has looked back to ask how the ruling class for seven centuries has become backward and less educated. Nor has anyone pointed a finger at either Sir Syed or at Mr Nehru.

Sociological Explanation of Backwardness:

Four Backward States: UP, Bihar, Bengal and Assam

Professor Max Weber, a renowned German sociologist and political theorist, had formulated a thesis, 'The Protestant Ethic'. His analysis showed that there was a close connection between interest and success in capitalist ventures and religious notions of the people. After detailed study, he had come to the conclusion that Protestants valued savings and their investments were routed in productive channels. Hence countries which were predominantly Protestants were industrially more advanced than others.

UP, Bihar, Bengal have been ruled by Muslims for centuries and the population of these areas has developed a conservative spirit in matters of capital enterprises. Agriculture was the main source of employment and livelihood. Those who owned land had no interest in improving the productivity. All savings made by the ruling and land-owning classes were spent on construction of luxurious houses and on enjoyment activities. The advent of the British rule brought about a sea change in the economic situation of these states. The British laid a network of railway lines and irrigation canals. As a result, industrial centres like Kanpur in UP, and in and around Calcutta developed in Bengal. Bihar and Assam also got an economic boost. Until the departure of the British in 1947, this region functioned as an engine of growth.

The fact that these States have not shown the deserved growth in the last 70 years indicates that entrepreneurship is missing. This in turn can be traced to the feudal mentality developed during the Muslim era. The widely accepted indicator of economic development, at present, is the level of per capital income. This is further supplemented by data on the share of industry in total Gross Domestic Product (GDP); recently, progress of States is also measured by Human Development Indices. Based on these yardsticks, it is seen that States like Uttar Pradesh, Bihar, West Bengal and Assam stand nowhere in comparison to Maharashtra, Gujarat, Tamil Nadu and Goa.

The story is no different in Islamic countries in the Middle East. A brief glance at the experience of overseas Islamic countries illustrates this.

Islamic Laws—the Bane of the Middle East

Professor Timur Kuran, Professor of Islamic Studies at Duke University in his book, *The Long Divergence: How Islamic Law Held Back the Middle East* has pointed to certain shortcomings in Islamic law that are responsible for the Middle East being not able to keep pace with the industrialisation of the Western countries. In particular, he has referred to: Islamic law of commercial partnerships; the Islamic inheritance system; the religious endowments system and the individualism of the Islamic law. During the first millennium, the Middle East was much ahead of the countries in western Europe. However, it suffered a decline in the second millennium for reasons mentioned above.

Institutions

Institution is a slippery concept that requires definition. By institution is meant a system of socially produced regularities that shape, and are in turn shaped by, individual behaviour.

An institution of great importance to Middle Eastern daily life was the holy law of Islam (sharia), also known as Islamic law. In principle, Islamic law covered all human activity. In the political discourse of the Ottoman Empire (1299 AD-1922 AD) there was even a category of laws known as ruler's law (*kanoon*), as distinct from Islamic law, and also a third category, customary law *(orf)*, which rested on precedent rather than religious scripture or learning. The two areas in which the Middle East fell conspicuously behind, right up to modem times were: People entered into contracts that followed an Islamic template and were enforced through Islamic courts. They apportioned estates according to Islamic inheritance rules. Residents of the region's great cities obtained services mostly from wakfs, which were trusts formed under Islamic law and supervised by officials with religious training. Almost all law suits involving at least one Muslim were litigated by

Muslim judges, under Islamic legal principles.

Cracking our puzzle thus requires close attention to the practical consequences of Islamic law. With respect to economic institutions, the eighth and ninth centuries saw the emergence of an Islamic law to govern the trusts known as wakfs as well as the refinement of the Islamic law of partnership. Successful imitation of foreigners required the transplantation of alien institutions, such as stock markets, municipalities, and laws supportive of large companies capable of outliving their founders.

Whereas commercial partnerships formed under Islamic law typically involved a few partners, who pooled resources for short-lived ventures, Westerners formed indefinitely lasting enterprises with tens, hundreds, and even thousands of shareholders by the 18th century. In traditional Middle Eastern credit markets, suppliers typically were individuals capable of making small loans. Westerners had access to commercial banks that could channel capital mobilised from the masses into large-scale productive ventures. No stock markets existed for trading shares of indigenous Middle Eastern companies, which tended to be ephemeral. Stock markets were gaining prominence in the West in the 20th century, where investors in long-living enterprises liquidated shares at will.

Supply of Social Services

The supply of urban social services offers another contrast. In the Middle East, the traditional provider was the wakfs. In the face of breathtaking technological advances, this form of trust proved inadequate as a vehicle for keeping services up to date. The municipality, a standard instrument of local governance in Western Europe, was better suited to the rapidly changing needs of cities. Institutions borrowed from the West were used also to limit Western influences, preserve old customs, and even invent new traditions.

Islamic Bank

From a historical perspective the concept of an 'Islamic bank' is a contradiction in terms. An Islamic bank operates on a scale far larger than any private enterprise the Middle East knew before the 19th century. It is a corporation, an organisation alien to Islamic law. Islamic banking thus constitutes an 'invented tradition'. Its architects have used Western institutional models not to make Muslim economic life more 'Western' but, rather, to encourage saving, investing, borrowing, and lending in ways at least cosmetically 'Islamic'. Their shared goal was to replicate specific Western achievements, not to appropriate Western culture indiscriminately.

Modern Economic Growth

By the mid-19th century, which marks the initiation of major reforms, the world had entered a new economic epoch, that of modern economic growth. Its chief characteristic is self-sustaining economic expansion at an unprecedented rate; although contractions can occur, they amount to temporary reversals along an upward path. If this is granted, it is simply a matter of record that until well after 1750 AD, considered the start of modem economic growth, the Middle East lacked the organisational forms and techniques.

Other Reasons of Underdevelopment

Freedom and Human Knowledge Deficits

The first Arab Human Development Report, issued in 2002 by a commission composed entirely of Arab thinkers, points to a 'freedom deficit' and a 'human capabilities/knowledge deficit' as two characteristics of the Arab world today. The former deficit refers mainly to governance patterns inimical to civil and political freedom and the latter to low educational attainment, access to information, and intellectual creativity. The Middle East has become a technological laggard, its states discouraged investment, its inhabitants were poorly educated, and its intellectual life lack vigour.

Technology and Organisational Capacity

In the 19th century, the Middle East was a laggard on both counts. It lacked the know-how essential for mass production as surely as it lacked a law of corporations. Britain, Germany, and France had both, which enabled their entrepreneurs to form huge companies capable of exploiting new technologies. Hence, Middle Eastern entrepreneurs had trouble competing in the global economy because of both technological and organisational stagnation. The absence of markets for trading company shares posed a more intractable obstacle to the Middle East's economic advancement than its delays in mechanising. Private organisational development versus' evolution of the state for institutions of governance are no easier to transplant than those of commerce or civil society.

Witness the Arab Middle East's persistently low international rankings relating to civil rights, government effectiveness, and rule of law, in spite of political reforms over the past century which has turned our gaze to segments of the social system beyond direct state control where stagnant practices become salient. Insofar as inertia explains the Middle East's failure to keep up with Europe, it is private economic life, not public administration, which calls for primary attention. To put it in terms of the tripartite legal categorisation familiar to historians, religious law and customary law merit analytic priority over the ruler's law.

Interactions with Other Regions

In discourses on why the Middle East became underdeveloped, a commonly articulated explanation points the finger at outsiders. The machinations of Europeans, Timur Kuran says, turned the region into a 'dependent','plundered', and 'self-doubting' part of the world. Still, interpretations that attribute the region's underdevelopment to foreign meddling miss vital ingredients of the historical record. Understanding the factors responsible for the West's dynamism will help to isolate obstacles to self-generated development in the Middle East. They will also elucidate why Islamic institutions well adapted to medieval conditions seemed impoverished a millennium later. The heart of the agenda is to examine the dynamics of private economic organisation in the pre-modern Middle East. Why critical transformations failed to occur is the question we seek to answer. Where the particulars involve religion, it is to religion that the argument must lead.

Unintended Secondary Consequences of Early Islamic Institutions

The Islamic inheritance system spread wealth by providing mandatory inheritance shares to all sons and daughters, and Islamic polygamy had the same effect by enabling the wealthiest merchants to have unusually numerous heirs. What could scarcely have been understood in the early Islamic centuries is that, in the face of outside developments, these institutions would eventually incapacitate Muslim merchants in their dealings with the West, in world markets, and even at partnership.

Madrasas

Over time the curriculum changed less in the madrasa than in the universities, helping to turn the Middle East into an intellectual backwater. Although many factors contributed to the region's lack of intellectual prominence after several bright centuries under Islamic rule, a basic cause lies in the wakfs' organisational limitations. Madrasas and universities were both non-profit organisations. The wakf became Islam's main organisational form for providing social services at a time when Western Europe deployed the corporation for many other ends.

The organisational gap widened in the late 16th century, when the West began applying the corporate form of organisation to profit-oriented production, finance, and commerce. In contrast, the universities of Paris and Oxford initially set up as trusts, in the 12th and 13th centuries, had become self-governing and self-renewing in due course.

Inheritance System

Islam's relatively egalitarian inheritance system raised the costs of liquidating a partnership prematurely, thereby limiting the size and duration of partnerships, fragmenting the estates of successful merchants, and hindering the preservation of businesses across generations. The dynamic consequences are critical here. Members of small and short-lived partnerships felt no urge to develop sophisticated accounting methods or to obtain greater liquidity through tradability. An unintended consequence of such stagnation is that the business community could not even contemplate using an organisational form akin to the corporation.

If the structural stagnation of commercial partnerships constituted one reason for the dearth of organisational innovation in general, another was that successful merchants tended to convert their wealth into real estate, for reconversion into the corpus of a wakf. They did so for the very reason why founding wakfs gained enormous popularity among high officials: the weakness of private property rights. Like other wealthy groups, prosperous merchants sheltered wealth within wakfs.

Why did the Middle East enter the 19th century as an underdeveloped region?

The critical deficiencies were: frozen wakf assets, atomistic financial markets, courts unsuited to impersonal exchange—none comprehended how such features were mutually reinforcing, or how they were blocking transformations essential to global competitiveness. Through wakfs, residents benefited from subsidised social services. Economic disputes were settled informally through arbitration or formally through courts that rendered judgments quickly. Islamic law was not considered harmful to economic progress. By the same token, the reasons why the Middle East fell behind remain a mystery still. To explain the lag in the region's modernisation, and Islam's role in this delay, we have had to focus on aspects of the Middle East's organisational heritage that turned into weaknesses gradually, through transformations elsewhere.

An Islamic partnership lacked entity shielding, in that any member could force its dissolution unilaterally, and its assets were exposed to demands from third parties. The death of partner terminated the partnership automatically, giving his heirs an immediate claim on a share of the assets; all surviving members incurred costs. The number of heirs could be large, because Islam's inheritance law assigns mandatory shares to designated relatives of the descendant. The partnership termination rule, like the lack of entity shielding, thus discouraged the formation of large and long-lived partnerships.

Merchants and investors would form small and short-lived partnerships in order to lessen the risks of untimely dissolution. In allowing polygamy, Islam compounded the incentives to keep partnerships atomistic and ephemeral. This is because merchants with multiple wives tended to have more heirs. Rarely did the business empires of the most successful merchants survive them, because their estates got divided into too many pieces to make recombination practical. Incentives to trade share were dampened. In sum, several self-enforcing elements of Islamic law—contracting provisions, inheritance system, marriage regulations jointly contributed to the stagnation of the Middle East's commercial infrastructure.

The Islamic inheritance system delayed organisational modernisation for a prime reason. The corporation was

Islamic Institutions that Helped Delay Economic Modernisation

Present in Islam's first few decades	Developed mostly or entirely after Islam's initial period
Inheritance system	Contract law
Acceptance of polygyny	Wakf
Ban of riba	Court system
Absences of corporation	Capitulations
Choice of law limited to non-Muslims	
Prohibition of apostasy	
Absence of merchant organisations	

precluded, and therefore, partnership remained the only possible starting point for developing durable and large commercial organisations.

The third of the seven problematic institutions present from the beginning, the ban on *riba*, an unjustified increment of interest rate, was a steady irritant to suppliers and users of credit. By requiring the use of stratagems, it raised credit costs. Although Islamic banks ostensibly do only interest-free business, in reality they give and take interest through means resembling the stratagems used in medieval financial markets. The Islamic legal system emerged without a concept of corporation contributed to keeping Middle Eastern businesses atomistic.

The fifth original institution was the choice of law. Allowing Islamic law to trump the legal systems of non-Muslims, and permitting anyone to sue in Islamic court at will depressed the competition faced by Islamic courts. Both the Quran and the remembered sayings of Prophet Muhammad contain references to apostasy as a religious offence. On the basis of these references, Muslim jurists of the 7th century declared apostasy punishable by death. The severity of this punishment doubtless contributed to the outcomes of Islamic legal pluralism.

To recapitulate, the question whether Islam's original institutions are compatible with modem economic life admits no categorical answer. Along with traditional institutions that are incompatible with economic success in the modern world, there are those that pose no significant problems. The Islamic inheritance system and its marriage regulations jointly hindered indigenous organisational modernisation, but once modern organisations were transplanted from the West, they ceased to harm economic performance.

Aligarh Muslim University—Cradle of Muslim Separatism

Jinnah described the Aligarh Muslim University (AMU) as an 'arsenal' of Muslim India. Professors Sayed Zafarul Hasan and Mohammed Afzal Qadri of AMU drew a detailed design for the partition of British India and worked out the geography of Pakistan which included present-day Indian territories like Hyderabad as well as Mysore State. No doubt, Aligarh was the ideological centre of Islamic ideas since its inception as the MohammedanAnglo-Oriental College. Justice MC Chagla and Rafiq Zakaria have referred to the UP Muslims as the 'cause' of Pakistan; according to them there would have been no Partition but for them. Prof M Mujeeb, Vice Chancellor of Jamia Milia Islamia also wrote at length to underline that but for the UP Muslims, there would have been no Pakistan.

The Mohammedan College named above, was founded in 1876. It gradually undertook the thought of separatism. In the year 1920, the college was upgraded to a university and it began to receive grant from the Government of British India. Despite its anti-national role, the government continued to increase its funding to AMU and now virtually all its expenses are met by New Delhi.

Not only professors but even the students went in large numbers to the Punjab to campaign for the Muslim League with its one-point programme of creating Pakistan in the

1945-46 elections. A sovereign country, if it is proud of its sovereignty, would have abolished the Aligarh institution on the morrow of Partition. But India has done the reverse by funding it generously and pampering it no less than doting parents. Sir Aga Khan, in his biography published in 1954, paid a handsome tribute to the work done by AMU for the creation of Pakistan. He recalls that the sovereign independent nation of Pakistan was born in the AMU.

In his efforts to further the interests of the Muslims of the Urdu speaking elite, Syed Ahmad Khan created a centre of Muslim political activity in India. In its infancy, the MAO College, Aligarh established in 1857 started publishing *Aligarh Institute Gazette* and the *Tahzib-ul-Akhlaq*. These publications were patronised by eminent Muslims like Syed Muhamud, Syed Ahmad's son, Chiragh Ali (the first native judge of the Alhabad High Court). Shibli and Hali whose Musadda (*The Rise and Fall of Islam*) was written at Syed Ahmad's behest awakened Muslims to the decline of their political influences.

Secondly, Syed Ahmad Khan founded the *Muhammadan Educational Conference* in 1886. By 1890, the name of the conference became Mohammedan Educational Congress. It was later on changed to Mohammedan Educational Conference. Eventually, it was changed to Mohammedan Anglo-Oriental Educational Conference. During the first twenty years of its existence (1886-1906), the work of the conference fell into two periods of almost equal length. Sir Syed was the secretary during the first ten years and in the next ten years, the post was held by Mohsin ul-Mulk.

The greatest achievement of the Conference was that of generating among Muslims sentiments of solidarity, says MS Jain author of the book, *The Aligarh Movement 1965*. During Sir Syed's lifetime there was a proposal to set up a Muslim University. The *Aligarh Institute Gazette* of 19th September 1901 states that the creation of a Mohammedan

University 'would give the Mohammedans more political power' than any political privileges they can possibly acquire.

The College and its attendant Conference were political organisations in all but name. The chief importance of the college was that it was the base from which UP Muslim elite groups led a Muslim political party in the province and in India.

The British rulers were quite aware of the pan-Islamic sympathies of Indian Muslims. In 1877 Lord Northbrook had told the House of Lords not only were there a disloyal portion of the Indian Mohammedans, but also religious Mohammedans, who *cannot be content with other than Mohammedan rule*. In 1882, Sir Alfred Lyall, Lt Governor of North-West Provinces and Oudh had written to the then Viceroy that there is little doubt that during the Egyptian War, the Indian Mohammedans were sympathetic to Arabi Beg. While describing a game of badminton in Delhi, Lyall wrote:

> 'Near me a Musalman, civil and mild, watched as the shuttlecocks rose and fell; and he said, as he counted his beads and smiled, God smite their souls to the depths of hell.'

Later, Sir Antony Macdonnell (1844-1925) noticed similar Muslim sympathies with the Turkish Sultan during the 1897 campaign.

The plain truth was that the Muslims were not trusted by the British rulers says Francis Robinson. *(Separatism among Indian Muslims,* Cambridge University Press, London, 1974).

Sir Syed—Father-figure of Pakistan

Syed Ahmad's contributions to the political cause of Indian Muslims are formidable. As a member of the Governor-General's Legislative Council from 1878, he successfully campaigned for *separate nomination of Muslims* to the local self-government institutions which were created by Lord Ripon. He was one of the original exponents of the two-nation theory and believed that Hindus and Muslims could not have an equal share in power. Syed Ahmad opposed the demands of the Indian National Congress for the enlargement of the representative government in India and the recruitment of Indians for government service by open competitive examination. In his view, representative government was inexpedient for a country inhabited by two different nations, Hindus and Muslims. (*Constitutional and Political History of Pakistan* by Hamid Khan)

Sir Syed reiterated his views later in his speeches made at Lucknow (28 September 1887) and at Meerut (16th March 1888). In Sir Syed's words: 'I come now to the main subject on which I wish to address you. That is the National Congress and the demands which that body makes of Government. In the time of Lord Ripon I happened to be a member of the Council. At that time the Local Boards and Municipality Bills were brought forward, and intention was that everybody should be appointed by election. The only person who was opposed to the system of election was myself. If I am not bragging too much, I may, I think, say that it was on account of my speech that Lord Ripon changed his opinion and made one-third of the members appointed and two-third elected (speech at Lucknow, 28th September 1887).

'I think it expedient that I should first of all tell you the reason why I am about to address you on the subject of tonight's discourse. You know, gentlemen, that for a long time, our friends, the Bengalis have shown very warm feelings on political matters. Three years ago they founded a very big assembly, which holds its sittings in various places, and they have given it the name National Congress. But my friends, the Bengalis have made a most unfair and unwarrantable interference with my nation, and therefore it is my duty to show clearly what this unwarrantable interference has been, and to protect my nation from the evils that may arise from it. Our Mohammedan nation has hitherto sat silent. But they have now been wrongly tampering with our nation. They even did not hold back from offering the temptation of money. Where is the man that does not know this? Who does not know who were the three or four Mohammedans of the North-West Provinces who took part with them, and why they took part? The simple truth is they were nothing more than hired men. And I want to show this that except Badruddin Tyabji who is a gentleman of very high position and for whom, I have great respect, no leading Mohammedan took part in it. He did take part, but I think he made a mistake.

'Now, suppose that all English and the whole English army were to leave India, taking with them all their cannons and their splendid weapons and everything, then who would be the rulers of India? Is it possible that under these circumstances two nations—the Mohammedans and the Hindus—could sit on the same throne and remain equal in power? Most certainly not.' (Speech at Meerut, 16th March 1888.)

BR Nanda, former Director of the Jawaharlal Nehru Museum and Library, quotes Bashir Ahmad Dar (*Religious Thoughts of Sayyad Ahmad Khan;* Lahore 1957) to the effect: 'Pakistan is in reality, the direct result of the whole scheme of things as envisaged by this good old man (Sir Sayyad); who represented in his person the ideology and aspirations of the whole Muslim nation of this subcontinent.'

The Hindi-Urdu Controversy

After Syed Ahmad Khan's death in 1898, two prominent Muslims played a leading role in the political awakening and formation of the All India Muslim League. They were: Syed Mehdi Ali, generally known by his Hyderabadi title Nawab Mohsin-ul-Mulk. He was born at Etawah, UP in 1887. The other was Mushtaq Husain also known by his Hyderabadi title of Nawab Viqar-ul-Mulk. He was born in District Moradabad, UP. On 18th April 1900, Sir Antony MacDonnell, Lt Governor UP, ordered the use of Hindi in place of Urdu. The majority of the population was Hindu. They had found it difficult to approach the administration for lack of knowledge of Urdu. Mohsin-ul-Mulk organised protest meetings against the government's order. 'For Muslims, Urdu is a dear possession, next in importance to Islam alone', says SM Ikram (*Modern Muslim India,* 1950). MacDonnell rushed to Aligarh and at a meeting of the Trustees of the College, he warned that if this public expression of views against government policy continued, the College would lose all assistance from the government. The agitation came to an end thereafter.

Foundation of the All India Muslim League

While introducing the Indian Budget in the House of Commons in 1906, John Morley, Secretary of State referred to the extension of representative elements in the Legislative Council. Immediately, in August 1906, Mohsin-ul-Mulk wrote to Archibald, Principal of Aligarh College, to inquire from the Viceroy as to whether he would like to receive a Muslim deputation for submission of a memorandum. Mohsin-ul-Mulk also wrote to Sir Ali Imam of Patna, Justice Shah Din of Lahore and Nawab Imad-ul-Mulk of Hyderabad to help him in drafting the memorandum. The deputation comprised thirty-five eminent Muslims, including, His Highness the Aga Khan, leader of the deputation. The memorandum was submitted on 1st October 1906.

The most important demands were for the nomination election of Muslim representatives to legislative council and municipalities through separate electoral colleges; employment of a due proportion of Muslims in government services and judiciary and establishment of a Muslim University. Viceroy Minto agreed to separate electorates but did not respond to the demand for a Muslim University and Civil and High Court appointments. After the deputation work was over, Nawab Mohsin-ul-Mulk and Nawab Viqar-ul-Mulk got busy with the formation of a political organisation. On 30th December 1906, at an annual session of the All-India Muslim Educational Conference at Dacca, an All India Muslim League was set up. Poet Hali paid his tribute to Nawab Mohsin-ul-Mulk at the next session of the Mohammedan Educational Conference held at Karachi in the following words: 'He (Mohsin-ul-Mulk) was a benefactor of the people, a friend of the Muslim. He fell a martyr—but not before the battle had been won.'

Role of UP Muslims

The Aligarh Movement, the central factor of Islamic renaissance in India, had two very important results. It was the first step towards the integration of Indian Islam. It was the Aligarh man who spearheaded the Muslim movement in every corner of India. In the second place, Aligarh elevated Urdu to the position of a national language for Indian Islam. Thus provided with a separate language and special ideology, the Muslims were able, in due course, to claim to be a separate nation. From a separate electorate (in 1909) to Pakistan was but an easy natural evolution, says KM Panikkar, an eminent historian (*Survey of Indian History,* 1947).

In this context, Professor Francis Robinson observes: 'UP Muslims on the other hand were at the heart of Muslim separatism. They mainly founded, and with the exception of the Bombay-based Jinnah, mainly led the organisation which represented the Muslim interest in Indian politics. In 1906, a large number of Muslims from the UP flocked to Dacca to found the All India Muslim League. Syed Ahmad Khan had founded in 1875, the Mohammedan Anglo-Oriental College at Aligarh which directed early Muslim political activity and nurtured many Muslim League politicians. He followed this with the establishment of the All-India Muslim Educational

Conference in 1886, which helped him impress his political will on Indian Muslims.'

In this organisation, the secretaryship was the most powerful position; and between 1906 and 1910 it was held by Muslims in Aligarh and between 1910 and 1926 by Muslims in Lucknow. After World War One, Muslims from the same province set up an association of Indian ulema and organised the Central Khilafat Committee. Professor Robinson goes on to say: 'In the League's years of glory from 1940 to Partition, UP Muslims were at the heart of the organisation, they headed the two most important posts after that of the President, and dominated its committees. Throughout the development of Muslim separatism in British India, whenever the politics of All India Muslim Organisations were vigorous, they were more the policies of UP Muslims than those of any other group of Indian Muslims.'

The Basis for Pakistan

In a speech delivered at a lunch hosted by Zia-ud-din Ahmad, Vice-Chancellor, Aligarh Muslim University on 8th March 1944, Jinnah said: 'Pakistan was not the product of the conduct or misconduct of Hindus. It had always been there, only they were not conscious of it. Hindus and Muslims though living in the same towns and villages had never been blended into a nation, they were always two identities. Pakistan started the moment the first non-Muslim was converted to Islam in India long before the Muslims established their rule. As soon as a Hindu embraced Islam, he was an outcaste not only religiously but also socially, culturally and economically. As for the Muslim, it was a duty imposed on him by Islam not to merge his identity and individuality in any other society. Throughout the ages Hindus have remained Hindus and Muslims have remained Muslims and they had not merged their identities. This is the basis for Pakistan.'

Syed Ahmad Khan had preached Hindu-Muslim unity from 1867 to 1884, until the implementation of Gladstonian liberal policies by Viceroy Ripon in India. He opposed the Indian National Congress in 1887 when the election of a Muslim, Badruddin Taybji as its President, appeared to him detrimental to the interest of the Muslims. In his anti-Congress speeches at Lucknow (1887) and Meerut (1888), he had declared that the withdrawal of the British would lead to chaos.

Role of AMU Students in the Creation of Pakistan

'We worked for Pakistan and played our part in making Allama Iqbal's dream a reality under the guidance of Qaid-e-Azam.' This is how a woman member of the Muslim Students Federation, UP summed up the role of students in the creation of Pakistan. In October 1939, the AMU Students Union passed a resolution condemning the fascist policies of the Congress government in the Provinces. Again in October 1941, the AMU students union passed a resolution to the effect:

'The best way to achieve India's freedom and to bring about lasting peace in the country is to strive for the establishment of Independent states as the regions of Hindus and Muslim majorities.' The Student Union went on to declare that Aligarh men are determined to hasten the realisation of this (Pakistan) ideal which, according to the Union, represents the universal faith of the Musalmans of India and it was the official creed of the Union. The Union is the centre to train the Muslim youth to play their role worthily in the Muslim national movement. Addressing the students on 31st August 1941, Liaquat Ali Khan declared: 'We look to you for every kind of ammunition to win the battle of independence of the Muslim nation.' In 1945, the *Aligarh Magazine* published its first Pakistan edition.

In the 1945 elections, students of the union went out to Punjab, NWFP, Sind and Bengal provinces to canvass for the Muslim League. Thereafter, Muslim League ulema became a dominant political force in Punjab. The students mobilised support for Pakistan in the referendum held in 1947 in NWFP and Sylhet district of Assam. Kasim Razvi, the fanatic communal leader from Hyderabad, was an alumnus of the Aligarh Muslim University.

AMU Teachers' Role in Creation of Pakistan

Being dissatisfied with the working of the provincial autonomy under the 1935 Act, AMU Muslim scholars suggested a number of alternatives to the 1935 Act. The schemes were: of the poet Iqbal; of Chaudhary Rahmat Ali; and of Latif of Hyderabad. The Aligarh scheme was that British India should be divided into three independent sovereign states: (a) a Muslim state of North-West India comprising Punjab, Sind, NWFP and Baluchistan to be known as Pakistan (b) a Muslim state of Bengal, Sylhet district of Assam and Purnea District of Bihar to be known as a 'Muslim Federation' and; (c) the rest of British India was to be called Hindustan. Within Hindustan, Delhi and Malabar (Kerala) were to be autonomous provinces and lastly, Hyderabad including Berar and Carnatic was to be a sovereign Muslim state. In short, the Aligarh scheme envisaged partition of British India into four states; three Muslim and one Hindu. After this, the Muslims in Hindustan were to be recognised as a separate nation. Little wonder, Qaid-e-Azam Jinnah paid handsome compliments to the students of the AMU for their role in the campaign for Pakistan in these words: I have been following the wonderful work that the Aligarh boys have done. You have proved what I said, that Aligarh is the arsenal of Muslim India. (*Students' Role in the Pakistan Movement* by Mukhtar Zaman, Karachi, 1978.)

Views of Sir Aga Khan

It was Sir Aga Khan who had led the Muslim delegation to Viceroy Minto in 1906 and asked for a separate electorate for

Muslims, reservation of jobs for Muslims and the establishment of a Muslim university. Later in his autobiography published in 1954, Sir Aga Khan observed the following about AMU: 'Often in a civilised history, a university has supplied a springboard for a nation's intellectual and spiritual renaissance. Aligarh is no exception to this rule. We may claim with pride that Aligarh was the product of our own efforts and of no outside benevolence; and surely it may also be claimed that the independent, sovereign nation of Pakistan was born in the Muslim university of Aligarh.'

In regard to the demand for the above university, the Collector of Aligarh, WS Marris wrote in his note of 17th May 1911: 'Aligarh is destined to be the focus of all Mohammedan intelligence and activity in India.' The Collector warned the government that the demand for the university began as a defensive move which is now acquiring an offensive character.

Integration

The foregoing pages have reviewed Hinduness, including its potential to help achieve peace in the world. However, its greater priority must surely be to bring about a lasting harmony in its home country. The age old egregious alienation in India is the one between the Hindus and Muslims. It is important to consider how Hinduness can play a role in ending this conflict. Doing so should be India's first priority, not simply for the sake of social peace but equally or perhaps more so for economic progress. The country's most backward part is the long belt beginning with UP in the west, going on to Bihar, Bengal and Assam. Incidentally, this belt comprises the greatest number of Muslims.

It is essential to iterate here that Hindu-Muslim riots were not coeval with the British, as Gandhi used to say. He claimed that this particular religious conflict would be a phenomenon of the past as soon as the British left India. This was, to begin with, a belief of either convenience or ignorance or both.

Hindu-Muslim conflict actually began soon after the

advent of Muslim invaders from the North, particularly when Mahmud of Ghazni kept coming, looting, enslaving and desecrating temples (between AD 1000-1027). The period of Ghaznavid raids on Hindus was followed by Mohammad Ghori's entry and entrenchment in India, paving the way for the Islamic Delhi Sultanate and a string of Muslim dynasties culminating with the Mughals. As the state was Islamic, the fear of violence that could be unleashed by the ruler understandably discouraged Hindus from hitting back. They had to absorb the invaders' shocks and suffer their effects. Thus, till the Muslims ruled, there were hardly any riots.

Hindu-Muslim riots of the kind we witness today on a significant scale did not begin until after the neutral British took over. This phenomenon has continued even after Independence; riots did not cease, as Gandhi had presumed. Many political parties, state as well as central, have believed that to win elections, it was necessary to pamper Muslims. It is only since 2014 that the situation is beginning to change.

An episode from the 18th century suffices to flagmark that the silent hostility between the two communities very much existed. Bengal chafed under the rule of Nawab Siraj-ud-Daulah, who ruled from Murshidabad. Some merchant princes of Bengal, led by Raja Naba Krishna Deb, who were fed up with the nawab's rule learnt that the East India Company had asked Robert Clive to proceed from Madras to Calcutta. They guessed that his mission was to teach Siraj-ud-Daulah a lesson for having humiliated the Company's establishment at Calcutta a few months earlier. The Raja and his friends believed this to be their opportunity to ensure the nawab's defeat and deposal. Naba Krishna Deb and his associates took the initiative to wean away the nawab's top general, Mir Jafar, and persuade him to remain inactive on the battlefield in order to facilitate Clive's victory. Mir Jafar's reward was to be the nawabhood of Bengal in place of the deposed nawab. Similarly, some others among

Siraj-ud-Daulah's military lieutenants too were persuaded to not fight.

The result was the outcome of the famous Battle of Plassey in June 1757, fought not far from Murshidabad. Clive's 3,500 soldiers and sepoys polished off the nawab's one lakh strong army long before sunset. This Hindu project of ending the nawabi rule succeeded resoundingly. Naba Krishna Deb and friends knew Clive could do what a Hindu alliance had till then failed to achieve. In any case, the neutral rule of the Christian British was any time better than the Muslim tyranny. The Company forced the erstwhile Muslim rulers, as it were, to sit on the same floor that the Hindus sat on. After centuries, the playing field at last was made level for both the communities. The Durga Puja festival came with the advent of autumn in 1757. For the first time in Bengali memory, it was publicly celebrated in the sprawling bungalow of Raja Naba Krishna Deb. And who was the chief guest at that celebration? None other than Robert Clive! (*Kolikata Ekaler O Sekaler*, Harisadhan Mukhopadhay, Publisher: P M Bagchi & Co Pvt Ltd.)

As time wore on, the polity changed and opportunities arose, Hindus took advantage, especially in the field of education. In contrast, Muslims under the spell of their maulavis mostly kept away from studying English as well as Western science. Gradually, the importance of the Persian language declined. In the bargain, Muslims fell back and Hindus forged ahead. These developments had their effects on the careers of the young men belonging to the two communities, a grievance still nursed by Muslims, at least in India.

The years 1857-58 witnessed the great rebellion, popularly called the Mutiny whose epicentre was UP. The cataclysm was largely led by the nawabs and other Muslim princes whose regimes had collapsed, or faced imminent collapse with the advent of the British. They had been largely in power before the arrival of this European power and therefore had the primary motivation to rebel. It was not surprising therefore, that British anger was largely directed towards Muslims. It is believed that 90 per cent of those hanged by the East India Company at Delhi Gate belonged to their community. Sir Syed Ahmad Khan had sided with the Company and helped to save many British lives. In due course, he realised how much his people had suffered over the previous century between forsaking good education and arousing bitter enmity. To facilitate a recovery, he founded an English school at Aligarh which later morphed into the Aligarh Muslim University. It was a person of Syed Ahmed Khan's eminence who could not help spontaneously declaring that the Hindus and Muslims were two separate nations, way back in 1888 at Lucknow. Syed sowed the seeds of Partition in 1947.

Yet the communal division of the country, expensive as it was in human blood and suffering, brought about no amity and harmony between the Hindus and Muslims. Although Jawaharlal Nehru and his progeny were born among Hindus, they pampered Muslims endlessly. This was probably because up to 90 per cent of the Muslims voted at election time, often *en masse*, while Hindus often polled as little as 40 per cent, or at times, even lower. In return, most prime ministers gave the minorities—a euphemism for Muslims—a virtual blank cheque. So much so, that many an aware Hindu felt as if the Muslim lobby had a veto on any Indian policy. If anything was disapproved by the Maulanas, it was not pursued by the government.

Even the Vajpayee government, between 1998 and 2004 followed a similar line. A glaring example of the veto was the way a Supreme Court judgment in the Shah Bano appeal for alimony of a few hundred rupees was overturned by the Rajiv Gandhi regime using his party's overwhelming majority in Parliament to pass the regressive Muslim Women's Bill in 1986. The prime minister did not have any scruples about himself asking one of his ministers, Arif Mohammad Khan, to support the apex court judgment, which was done eloquently and he resigned over the issue. So crucial was the Muslim support to the Congress party, harnessed by the Maulanas.

Jawaharlal Nehru had shown his pro-Muslim bias very early in independent India. Articles 25 to 30 (ostensibly to protect minority rights), which were drafted to persuade the Muslims not to press for Partition, were persevered even after the division of the country. Soon after Independence, the princely states, the *zamindari* and *jagirdari* systems were abolished. But the wakfs were left untouched, although they were lands confiscated by Muslim invaders and redistributed to their supporters. Wakfs have been nationalised or dissolved in Turkey, Egypt and many other Islamic countries. The pinnacle of pampering was attained by former Prime Minister Manmohan Singh when he repeatedly declared 'Muslims First' and promised them the first 15 per cent of the country's resources.

This chasm has to be closed sooner than later if all Indian citizens are to put their shoulder to the wheel of progress. To restate, Partition should have been a final solution.

Unfortunately, it was not allowed to be by the leaders at the time, whether Gandhi, Nehru and the others. It is never too late, as they say, provided there is a will amongst the leaders today. The people have to be told the truth about Partition, how the country was divided only on the basis of religion: Pakistan for Muslims and India for the rest. Hindus have been all but ethnically cleaned out of Pakistan, with barely 3 per cent left there. As much as 75 per cent of Hindus have been driven out from what is Bangladesh since 1971. The story of Hindu persecution continues even today, with the ethnic cleansing of Kashmir's Hindus by the state's Muslim majority since 1989 being only a new chapter in this continuing grim saga.

The problem of Muslim separatist mentality is compounded by the twin factors of the feeling of some imagined superiority over the Hindus and the creation and activity of Pakistan, a state whose very birth is based on hatred for Hindus.

Muslims, long accustomed to being the rulers of India for a better part of 500 years or so, failed to quell Hindu resistance and revival and subsequently lost out to the Marathas and later the British. The feeling of defeat at the hands of a people who were once their subjects has been galling along with their sheer inability to cope with the demands of the changes civilisation has wrought can be imagined. Little wonder then, that the Muslim mind keeps harking to a long lost past, one that will never be restored. This mindset makes itself manifest in the form of communal riots, tension with Hindus and in recent years, terrorism, aided and abetted by Pakistan, whose one-point *raison d'être* is war against kafir India.

Hijrat, Migration a Peaceful Option

Tragically, because of the brainwashing in their madarsas, Muslims who are Indian by blood continue to perceive themselves not as the offspring of the same Indian soil as Hindus are, but as descendants of Islamic invaders from West and Central Asia who attacked Hindus, destroyed their places of worship, enslaved them and ruled over Hindustan. Thus, it is no surprise at all that it is individuals like Mahmud of Ghazni and Alamgir Aurangzeb who continue to be role models for most Muslims of the subcontinent even today.

The time has come to tell the Muslims in India to look upon Dara Shikoh, the eldest son of Mughal emperor Shah Jahan and Mumtaz Mahal, as an ideal role model rather than Aurangzeb, the third son of the same parents. Dara was not unfaithful to Islam, the Prophet and the Quran, but he rightly had space in his mind and heart for others, Hindus or otherwise. He admired Sufism for its liberalism and the scope it offered for spiritualism, whereas Aurangzeb was the opposite; a bigoted Muslim who had no sympathy for kafirs or non-believers in

Allah. Breaking idols and desecrating temples was intrinsic to him, perhaps more so than governing his empire. We have to tell the Muslims in India that it is for them to choose. They can choose the example of Dara Shikoh and mingle with the mainstream of the country.

If not, and they prefer the Aurangzeb way, let them be good momins (faithful Muslims) in a Dar-ul-Harb (land of conflict) and undertake hijrat (migration) out of India. They can go either to Pakistan, Bangladesh or any other Dar-ul-Islam of their choice. The Government of India should approach Islamic countries like Saudi Arabia, Libya or any other country that has plenty of land area and request them to allot some land for the migration or hijrat of Muslims out of India. Every adult (above 18 years) ought to be made to sign an affidavit to solemnly confirm his or her choice between the two alternatives, Dara Shikoh or Aurangzeb, and their commitment to fight for India even if the enemy is Muslim. Such a declaration must also include a signature favouring the return of those masjids which were unquestionably temples. In any case, Islam does not permit ibadat (worship) where there was earlier a place of worship of another religion.

Compulsory Voting

In this context, a plea should be made to Election Commission and the other powers that be is to make voting in election to Parliaments and State Assemblies *compulsory*. Many an electoral deviation would get straightened out. For example, vote bank politics or appeasing a section of people to win elections. In Gujarat up to 1990 or so the prevalent belief among political workers was up to 90 per cent Muslims voted when the total voting average used to be around 50 or less. This meant that a Muslim was worth some two votes in contrast to the Hindus one. If almost everyone voted, this deviation from democracy would cease.

Compulsory voting is not a novel idea. It was introduced in Australia for an election in 1915. By 1942, in all federal elections casting a vote was compulsory for all eligible citizens. For years now, only about 5 per cent voters fail to poll. People in this situation are asked to explain their failure to vote. If no satisfactory reason is provided (for example, illness or religious prohibition), a fine of up to $170 is imposed, and failure to pay the fine may result in a court hearing and additional costs. The immediate justification for compulsory voting at the federal level was the low voter turnout (59.38%). The 1925 federal election was the first to be conducted under compulsory voting, which saw the turnout figure rise to 91.4%. The turnout increased to about 95% within a couple of elections and has stayed at about that level since. This is one measure that would enable Muslims to integrate with mainstream India.

In this regard, immediate and timely action by responsible Muslim leaders who have a stake in their community's future will be important. Their role will be crucial. Political and administrative actions have their limitations in tackling social problems.

Political Action

In the Indian context, given its socio-cultural history, the ground for political action too will have to be prepared by determined and relentless efforts on the social and educational plane. The problem of communalism as it exists today in India is undeniably an outcome of Islam, which is monolithic and theocratic by its very nature. However, the march of history is testimony to the fact that the most powerful theocracies sooner or later consume themselves, which is an inexorable process. Global perception of Islam has begun changing sharply after the 11 September 2001 Islamic terror attacks on the Twin Towers in New York in the USA. Further acts of Islamic terrorism, particularly in India and the West, have only further hardened attitudes towards

Islam, with the turn of global events clearly pointing towards the building up of a major conflagration between the freedom-loving world and that of the denizens of cult of the desert. It is for the Muslims to make their choice—whether to abandon their religio-cultural revanchism and join the mainstream of humanity, or cling to their medieval obscurantism with its inevitable outcome. No religion or ideology is an exception to this diktat of time, which is something that must be driven home relentlessly into the Muslim mind, to bring about true and lasting integration.